Metaphor
& Public Communication

Metaphor & Public Communication

*Selected Speeches of
Lee Kuan Yew
&
Goh Chok Tong*

*Ong Siow Heng
& Nirmala Govindasamy-Ong*

Graham Brash
Singapore

© Dr. Ong Siow Heng &
  Nirmala Govindasamy–Ong, 1996

First published in 1996 by
Graham Brash (Pte) Ltd
32 Gul Drive
Singapore 629480

ISBN 981-218-056-7
All rights reserved

Typeset by Syarikat Broadway Typesetting Sdn. Bhd.
Printed in Singapore by General Printing Services Pte Ltd

For

Benjamin Joshua Jie-Ming Ong

and

Deborah Joy Ming-Hwei Ong

Acknowledgements

We are grateful to many people for this book, especially the following:

Gael Lee, Mosman Ismahil and Teng Fang Yih at Graham Brash for their keen editorial skills and valuable help;

The National University of Singapore for kindly assisting with the cover of the book; and

our children, Benjamin and Deborah, for their patience, understanding and encouragement.

Ong Siow Heng
Nirmala Govindasamy-Ong

Contents

Preface

1. The Meaning of Metaphor   1
    Treatment of Metaphor
    Introduction
    Aristotle
    Cicero & Quintillian
    Modern Philosophy
    Early 20th Century Positivist Criticism of Metaphor
    A System of Metaphoric Concepts
    Summary
    How Metaphor Works
    Introduction
    Epiphor or Metonymy
      Substitution & Comparison Views
    Diaphor or Metaphor
      Interaction View
    Metaphorical Contexts & Intensional Contexts
    Summary
    Method of Analysis of Metaphor in Featured Speeches
    Glossary of Technical Terms

2. The Communist Threat
   (Middle to Late 1950s)   40
    Historical Background
    "How The Communists Operate"

  Speech
  Metaphoric Analysis
  Summary of Analysis
 "Envoy From The Underground"
  Speech
  Metaphoric Analysis
  Summary of Analysis

3. **The Merger and Separation of Singapore and Malaya (1963–1965)**   67
 Historical Background
 "Are There Enough Malaysians To Save Malaysia?"
  Speech
  Metaphoric Analysis
  Summary of Analysis

4. **Consolidating & Moving Ahead (1964–1965)**   100
 Historical Background
 Speech on Eve of National Day, 8 August 1966
  Speech
  Metaphoric Analysis
  Summary of Analysis

5. **The Economic Recession and Recovery (1985–1986)**   118
 Historical Background
 "The Gordian Knot"
  Speech
  Metaphoric Analysis
  Summary of Analysis
 "Economic Recovery, Education and Jobs"
  Speech
  Metaphoric Analysis

Summary of Analysis
"The Long March"
Speech
Metaphoric Analysis
Summary of Analysis

Conclusion 179

Index 182

Preface

This book is a study of the use of metaphor in public address. Specifically, it focusses on key speeches made during various periods in Singapore's history.

The decision to focus on local speeches was deliberate as most local speeches have not been analysed. In textbooks on speech criticism, the model speeches have always come from the West. While many Western speeches are interesting in their form and development, local speeches are not lacking in these qualities. A study of some important local speeches will:

- show how the speakers adapted their messages to their social context,
- illustrate what makes metaphors effective, and
- encourage appreciation for public address in Singapore.

Why are metaphors the object of scrutiny here? Metaphors are an important aspect of rhetoric. Many scholars and theorists, among them linguists, philosophers, scientists, theologians and artists postulate that metaphors play a persuasive and cognitive role in urging audiences toward action. Metaphors may sometimes be an embellishment, but more than that, they have an inherent power to persuade.

The first goal of this book is to study the metaphors that were used to describe certain periods of crises and consolidation in Singapore's past, as well as those metaphors that were used to persuade and inspire the nation to overcome them. It is significant that the speeches chosen for this book were delivered by the former and current premier of Singapore. An examination of the metaphors in their speeches will illustrate their able leadership in helping the nation sail through difficult storms. Thus, this book focusses on several major speeches made during the periods of:

- the Communist Threat (middle to late 1950s),
- Singapore's merger with Malaya (1963–1965),
- Singapore's subsequent consolidation as a nation (1964–1965), and
- the economic recession and recovery of 1985–1986.

Secondly, this book hopes to exhort those engaged in public discourse to craft and invent metaphors with care to persuade their case.

Thirdly, as we look forward to meeting the perpetual challenge of improving the social, cultural and economic aspects of life in Singapore, we need to collectively discover and re-invent metaphors that will inspire and sustain us. Any kind of discourse or rhetorical stylistics is intrinsically tied to the improvement of civic life. Metaphor is to be discovered and reinvented not just for the sake of embellishment, but for persuasion and the inspiration of the populace.

In the first chapter, we provide a brief history of metaphor's turmoil and resurgence in academia. This history of metaphor is necessary in order to underline metaphor's potential to persuade. It also highlights the fact that metaphorical analysis is a legitimate tool for appreciating and studying discourse.

Subsequent chapters will analyse the types of metaphors used in critical speeches made by Singapore's prime ministers. Perhaps not all readers' views will coincide as to the choice of what constitutes a key speech or critical period in local history. This book does not insist on such concurrence. Rather, the aim of the analysis is to focus on the metaphors, not engage in debate on the characteristics of critical periods.

1. The Meaning of Metaphor

Treatment of Metaphor

Introduction | A review of the literature on the theory of metaphor will help us come to some conclusion about how metaphor works.
    Metaphors are commonly encountered and easily recognised. They are often used in ordinary speech without any consciousness by the user. But metaphors have a chequered reputation in Western philosophical circles. Difficulties arise when philosophers try to define metaphors and explain how they work or attempt to circumscribe their role in human communication and thought. Opinions differ over whether metaphor is at the aesthetic periphery of communication or belongs at the centre of epistemological and ontological discussion.

Aristotle | The first extensive treatment of metaphor by a philosopher was by Aristotle in *Rhetoric*[1] and *Poetics*.[2] He evaluated metaphor as having a significant role in poetry to provide knowledge through mimesis, and to persuade an argument in rhetoric. Strangely enough, however, his comments and his definition of metaphor laid the groundwork for some of the later maligning that metaphor suffered.

Aristotle defined metaphor as "giving the thing a name that belongs to something else" or a "transference" of the name from "genus to species or from species to genus, or from species to species, or on grounds of analogy".[3] This initial definition of metaphor as a name being transferred from an original application to a secondary application paved the way for subsequent thought on metaphor centred on words, taken in isolation, rather than on how metaphors function as part of the whole system of linguistic communication and thought process. This resulted in the impression that metaphors serve as artifice, synthetically wrought, because a word actually names only one thing and that thing is the meaning of that word. The implication, as noted by some later philosophers, was that an adequate examination of language and communication could be conducted at the level of individual words as if a sentence is the sum total of its individual words and as if the basic semantic unit* is only the word.

*Please see Glossary of technical terms at end of Chapter 1.

As a result, philosophical reflection on metaphor has tended to lean towards the idea of metaphor as deviance from what is strictly necessary for communication, or what is strictly true. This was another effect of Aristotle's view of metaphor as something that "deviates from ordinary modes of speech".[4] Usually taken to mean deviance from literal usage, this definition of metaphor permitted the later distrust of metaphor as changing the meaning of words. Language came to be thought of in a dichotomy of terms, literal language for logic and figurative language for effect. Little attention was focussed on how the two functioned together in all communication. This distinction coloured all later thought on language and human thought and communication.

Aristotle also referred to metaphor as being based on "an intuitive perception of the similarity in dissimilars".[5] This had the unfortunate effect of preventing future consideration of metaphor as something more complex than or at least different from simile. It discouraged the idea that metaphor can hinge on differences rather than similarities between things compared. Aristotle saw metaphor and simile as very much alike: "the difference is but slight . . . they are really the same thing."[6] The assumption is that the transfer of name from one thing to another is based on some quality that the two have in common, so that comparison is possible.

Aristotle saw metaphors as useful for setting "the scene before our eyes" so that we can "get hold of new ideas" by stretching the imagination.[7] But he emphasized the basic similarity or resemblance necessary to make a metaphor work: "metaphors must be drawn . . . from things that are related to the original things."[8] Unfortunately, instead of focussing on the complexity of metaphors, future considerations of language tended to assume that metaphor always work simply as simile.

Aristotle also stressed that metaphor is used appropriately when it "gives style, clearness, charm, and distinction as nothing else can."[9] This drew attention to metaphor's role in embellishing and lending style rather than imparting content. Many who came after Aristotle tended to hold the view that metaphor was merely decorative. They implied that metaphor can be rephrased in literal language without any loss of its cognitive content.

Also, when Aristotle wrote that metaphor is used inappropriately, ie. in a way that it does not "fit", he was implying that metaphor cannot or should not be used to convey novel ideas about a thing. These would not "fit" or "correspond", implying that all ideas of similarity are already in our minds and that metaphor only draws attention to these.[10] This view that metaphor cannot communicate innovative or essential information is unequivocally expressed in Aristotle's warning against using metaphors in definitions because "a metaphorical expression is always obscure,"[11] the implication being that metaphors are not lucid and can lead one to error in judgement.

Cicero and Quintilian

Cicero, like Aristotle, saw metaphor as emphasizing a resemblance between two words.[12] In fact, both Cicero and Quintilian[13] saw simile as superior to metaphor. However, it should be remembered that Cicero and Quintilian were not providing an anatomy or physiology of metaphor, but were addressing the teaching of oratory. Indeed, although they mentioned metaphor only in the context of how tropes* can facilitate rhetoric, we cannot conclude that they considered metaphor to have limited value. In fact, Quintilian said:

the changes involved concern not merely individual words, but also our thoughts and the structure of our sentences. In view of these facts, I regard those writers as mistaken who have held that tropes necessarily involve the substitution of word for word.[14]

Notwithstanding these views, in writing of effective oratory, Quintilian and Cicero wrote of metaphor as embellishment or ornament, with no distinctive cognitive function.

Modern Philosophy

Despite what might be construed as Aristotle's deprecation of metaphor, he appreciated many aspects of metaphor, such as its capacity to name that which has not been named. He noted that there is no term for the scattering of light by the sun, "but as this is related to the sun, as sowing is to the scatterer of seed, we have the expression 'sowing the god created flame' ".[15]

Aristotle was also aware that metaphor is related to sound judgement and understanding, as metaphor is the only poetic device "that cannot be learnt from anyone else, and it is a sign of natural genius, as to be good at metaphor is to perceive resemblances".[16] But up to the mid-20th century, the prevailing impact of Aristotle's writings about metaphors was not in fact as well-balanced as his own writings were.

The assumption that metaphors work by persuasive charm or appeal to the aesthetic or affective and are thereby inferior to persuasion by bare logic, was one by-product of the

Greek philosopher's views on metaphor. One effect of the popularity of the idea that language has two functions, cognitive (for making objective statements) and emotive (for style and persuasion) was the view that metaphors are not essential for communicating truth or logic as whatever is phrased metaphorically can be phrased literally. This view presumes that language is not a complex rhetorical system of cooperation between literal and metaphorical language but rather the passing on of logic from one person to another. As Edie expresses it:

> the problem of the metaphorical... aspect of language is perhaps most perplexing, vexed, and intractable question in the whole of the philosophy of language. It brings us to the pivotal centre of the distinction between language as a 'system' and language as 'a speech act', ie. the distinction between language used for 'logic' and 'rhetoric'.[17]

In modern philosophy, the empiricists' devaluing of metaphor was predominant. The attitude towards metaphor could well have been summed up by Hobbes when he said that metaphors use words for other than their proper purpose. To him, the proper purpose of words is to give form to thoughts and knowledge, dredge them from memory and express them to others.[18] Metaphorical language distorts communication because metaphors are "senseless and ambiguous"[19] and use words "in other sense than that they are ordained for; and thereby deceive others".[20] This rationalist view is based on the belief that our thoughts and knowledge are acquired and passed on through literal language as it is precise. Metaphors confuse because they are a deviant use of words and therefore cannot make truth claims or statements of objective truth. Hobbes charged metaphors with causing "contention and sedition, or contempt"[21] because of ambiguity over what a metaphor might actually refer to, as the word is not used according to its dictionary definition.

One philosopher who held similar views to Hobbes was John Locke who criticised that "all the artificial ... application of words ... are for nothing else but to insinuate wrong ideas".[22] Hegel considered metaphor "a simple ornament" and an "accessory".[23] John S. Mill relegated metaphor to the role of a signpost to draw attention to an argument: "A metaphor then, is not to be considered an argument, but as an assertion that an argument exists."[24]

In other words, metaphors were thought to have no cognitive content beyond their literal paraphrase. Their purpose was assumed to be stylish embroidery that did not constitute the material of argument. The idea is that universally true propositions can communicate best in the absence of metaphors, which seem to only serve the function of distracting the reader.

This empiricist idea, however, is open to argument. It is only partially true and is certainly not applicable to all propositions.

While mathematics and formal logic use a very formalised and abstract language, mathematical language cannot fulfil the broader demands of communication. The way we communicate is an altogether wider experience involving the need to express individuality because that is how the world is experienced by each person, and this cannot be done through literal language alone. Even in mathematics and science, as Edie points out:

> there lies beneath the threshold of what is, strictly speaking, communicated differences of meaning both for the 'communicator' and for the 'receiver', although in mathematics and science these differences are minimal.[25]

In fact, even in science, much of the language is metaphorical as exemplified by the common expression "the movement of electrons". This compares electrons to particles that can be moved, whereas in fact this is merely a convenient way to speak of and imagine what happens at the subatomic level.

Although most philosophers turned their backs on metaphors, those associated with the arts saw them as a form of creativity transcending ordinary life. Metaphor became associated with art, religion and poetry, and disassociated from science.

This romantic embrace of metaphor is related to Rousseau's arguments on how language originated. His ideas are based on the belief that the human conceptual system is essentially metaphoric. He postulates that all language develops by the transfer of meaning, namely by figures. New discoveries are thus always tropes, referred to in old, existing terms. New terminology is invented for the new findings later, when these findings are more familiar because "one calls things by their true name only when one sees them in their true form."[26]

Nietzsche too, did not separate metaphor from literal language.[27] According to him, metaphoric understanding permeates all human thought and speech, and is thus essential to knowledge. Metaphor is the method by which we meet and deal with the world. Hence, what we know is necessarily known metaphorically. Words work multiple duties when the same word is used to refer to many similar things, eg. "fish" refers to so many aquatic creatures. In the sense that the same word has to fit so many things, it is metaphorical. Thus, our experience of the world is essentially metaphorical, "a mobile army of metaphors, metonymies, anthropomorphisms".[28]

He also did not limit metaphor to linguistic communication, but recognised it as the very medium by which we make sense of our experiences and relationship with our surroundings. What are cited as basic non-metaphorical truths are only "illusions of which one has forgotten that they are illusions; worn out metaphors which have become powerless to affect the senses".[29] For example, "stem of the wine glass", may once have evoked the image of "a flower on a stalk". Now it immediately brings to mind that part of the wine glass that we hold between our fingers. This is because the metaphor has become conventional over time. This aspect of Nietzsche's philosophy of equating the way humans think to metaphor was, however, not picked up by those with an empiricist bent.

Early 20th Century Positivist Criticism of Metaphor

The empiricist critique of metaphor led to the early 20th century positivist criticism of metaphor, specifically the idea that scientific knowledge can be transmitted by a system of literal and verifiable statements alone. Ogden and Richards, for example, stated that figurative language involves "the use of words to express or incite feelings and attitudes" – at that time assumed to be absent in scientific argument and enterprise. It is "using words merely to evoke certain attitudes as opposed to making an actual truth statement with literal language".[30] This implies that metaphor can be ignored as it has no important philosophical use. In other words, what metaphors mean can be more truthfully and simply expressed in literal paraphrase without any loss of cognitive import.

Edie interprets this attitude to metaphors as the stance that metaphors are a "weakness in human thought which could be avoided if only we were more astute and tried a little harder".[31] Even after this cognitive/emotive dichotomy was called into question as an oversimplification of how language functions, the positivist attitude about the superfluity of metaphor remained.

This tradition was challenged by I.A. Richards[32] and later Max Black.[33] Echoing

Nietzsche, Richards offered an alternative to the prevailing view of metaphors in his aptly named *The Philosophy of Rhetoric*. He attempted to claim a place for the study of metaphor in philosophy by showing that metaphors are ubiquitous in thought, not just emotions: "thought is metaphoric, and proceeds by comparison and the metaphors of language derive therefrom."[34] Thoughts develop and advance by making comparisons, so metaphors are by nature already present in our thinking process itself. Metaphor should thus be considered a principle of thought rather than of language alone.

Richards drew attention to the fact that language is essentially part of the human expression of existence. Language cannot be studied in isolation from the study of people as people use language to structure and interpret their experiences. Cognition and discovery are in this way dependent upon metaphor.

Richards also argued that metaphors are not the exception to the rule, or out of the ordinary. They are not aberrations of ordinary speech. This was a unique claim for metaphor in contrast to the commonly accepted Aristotelian view of deviation. Richards pointed out that metaphor is inextricably intertwined with all discourse and so it is impossible to communicate without metaphors.

Richards' views are all the more convincing if we recall that the empiricist Hobbes referred (p. 7), without apparent irony or humour, to certain meanings as being "ordained" for certain words. He wrote of making sense of metaphors as "wandering amongst innumerable absurdities" and that "metaphors... are like *ignus fatui*".[35] Thus, even in questioning the importance of metaphors, Hobbes seemed to have found figurative speech inescapable and certainly helpful.

Richards pointed out that metaphor was formerly assumed to be merely ornamental because of the unquestioning acceptance that metaphors carry no metaphysical or epistemological weight. But the very way the mind apprehends something new is to perceive, speak and think of it in terms of what is already known. The world as humans know it is a "projected world".[36] We are conscious of the world we live in, and project or express our experiences in whatever terms are available and which make sense to us. The metaphorical expressions we use are "superimposed upon a perceived world which is itself a product of an earlier or unwitting metaphor".[37] For example, "flow of electricity" compares electric current to movement of water. But this paradigmatic innovation has passed into common usage so we do not give it a second thought. When a metaphorical expression is composed such as 'when I met my hero, electricity coursed through my blood', this is a superimposition upon the perception of the metaphor of electricity as flowing. Such perceptions and/or metaphors are hidden or invisible which, through long use, have become powerless to suggest images and thus are no longer recognised as metaphorical.

Metaphors are grounded in common experience within a culture. A metaphor creates new perspectives, meaning or thoughts for existing ideas by presenting objects normally put in one category in another category. Thus, our imagination and understanding are stretched. This recategorizing has also been called "calculated category mistake".[38]

Having attempted to link the study of metaphor with the study of the human psyche, Richards also suggested how metaphors work. He regarded them as "two thoughts of different things active together and supported by a single word, or phrase, whose meaning is the resultant of their interaction".[39] The metaphorical meaning is thus the interaction of two different groups of thought about two different things, which interact with each other and produce meaning. This interaction is supported by one word or phrase. Hence, in "the world is a carnival", the two groups of thought comprising the metaphor are, in Richards' terms, the tenor* (the world) and the vehicle* (the carnival). Interaction between the two creates the resultant meaning. Interestingly, this resultant meaning is not necessarily the similarities between "carnival" and "world". The meaning could be based on dissimilarities to stimulate the audience's imagination. It also need not involve images (eg. colourful carnival). It can include ideas or concepts (e.g. a carnival is briefly exciting then unceremoniously over). Since the meaning is a result of this unique interaction of the two groups of thought, the metaphor cannot be substituted by literal paraphrase. If substitution is not possible, then metaphors are indispensable to human thought.

Later, Max Black made similar arguments for metaphor. Richards' rather extreme claims that all language is essentially metaphorical were slightly tempered by Max Black who argued that while some metaphors are not reducible to cognitively literal expressions, others are. To Richards, a common expression such as "leg of the table" is actively metaphorical. On the other hand, Black regarded it as a dead metaphor, easily substituted by "base/support of the table". But Black realised that some metaphors cannot be translated into literal terms. More startlingly, Black claimed, metaphors may not always just draw attention to existing similarities between things, but actually create new, never before apprehended similarities.

This idea of dead metaphors is arguable as it is not hard to imagine such metaphors being resuscitated and brought out at appropriate times. They would still be distinguishable from literal language (which was never a trope and never invented as clichés were). Danto argues that ordinary language cannot be considered solely as "a graveyard for defunct metaphors",[40] and that these resurrected metaphors cannot be substituted by a "precisification", whereby literal language is not necessarily a way to make metaphor supposedly more precise. Not all language is metaphorical; there are non-metaphorical structures of language.

The question of how metaphors should be defined, and how useful they are for formulating philosophical argument or finding the truth, remained influenced by Aristotle's views for future generations of philosophers. Beardsley suggested that a metaphor has a degree of literal inappropriateness, a "logical opposition".[41] This was his interpretation of Aristotle's "deviance from ordinary modes of speech", where deviance is ascribed to denomination only. There must be some twist or deviance in its expression so that it logically contradicts itself. Henle viewed a metaphor as a mismatch or "clash of literal meanings".[42] Goodman referred to this mismatch as a contraindication of terms.[43] On the whole, these philosophers based their statements on the semantically deviant nature of metaphors.

The problem with this basis is that it does not explain why sentences in certain contexts could be literally interpreted without being semantically deviant or have literal falsity, yet in other contexts can work as a metaphor. "I devoured my books" would be a literal remark made by an insect in a story about insects, but if said by a human student would be a metaphoric statement. So not all metaphors are semantically deviant; semantic deviance is not an indicator of a metaphor. A metaphorical expression could be both, literally and metaphorically accurate, depending on the context. For example, in "people who live in glass houses shouldn't throw stones", a metaphorical meaning would be indicated if a literal reading would not fit or would go against the rest of the context. This unsuitability is often referred to as a tension or strain between the literal sense of the statement and the surrounding situation.

Loewnberg offers the view of contextual deviance when a literal reading is tried but does not work.[44] Her view is based on the idea that a metaphor can only be properly recognised and its pertinence accounted for within its total context. Max Black calls this "the lack of congruence with the surrounding text and non-verbal setting."[45] But he also warns that "there is no infallible test for resolving ambiguity... in discriminating the metaphorical from the literal."[46] Johnson summarises these opinions on identifying metaphor as involving "some strain between the normal sense of the utterance and the total speech situation in which it occurs."[47] In other words, metaphorical utterances can be identified only if we take into account some knowledge possessed by speakers outside of the sentence and outside of their use of linguistic symbols.

The problem seems to go back to how deviance is to be defined. In Riceour's terms, the question is whether it is a deviant denomination* only or rather a deviant predication*, where the metaphor works because a word is applied to an unexpected subject. The metaphorical meaning is obtained by the lexical deviance*. This actually makes the metaphor a "paradigmatic deviance"* which is "precisely the kind of deviance described by classical rhetoricians". Riceour points out that classical rhetoric was not wrong, then, but only "described the 'effect of sense' at the level of the word while it overlooked the production of this metaphorical twist at the level of sense" which depends on the whole utterance.[48]

This idea of contextual deviance or incongruence seems to point, at least partially, in the direction of deviance being a factor of the sociolinguistic culture or milieu. The composer of metaphors is one who:

> from an inconsistent utterance for a literal interpretation, draws a significant utterance for a new interpretation which deserves to be called metaphorical because it generates the metaphor not only as deviant but as acceptable.[49]

A speaker analyses the character, values and cultural context of his audience. He fashions his speech according to his analysis such that they would recognise certain statements as literal and others as non-literal. The audience identifies something as a metaphor from their perception and understanding of the context, their own world view and their assumptions about the speaker. The speaker and the audience are thus personae in a dramatic, interactive exchange.

Edwin Black explains this interaction in terms of the composer and audience as personae who have certain expectations of each other, and who attribute certain qualities to each other.[50] Black thus emphasizes the idea that human communication is a dynamic enterprise rather than the mere passing on of static information in rigid, literal terms.

Once an experience has been named or labelled and then communicated to a particular linguistic community, that community is empowered with the terminology to hold that experience in its consciousness and refer to it as constituting part of their collective world view. To affirm this role that metaphor plays in the human psyche and language is to acknowledge that our intimacy with the world "is not static and juxtapositional but dynamic and dialectical."[51]

A System of Metaphoric Concepts

Lakoff and Johnson fine-tuned this view of dialectical dynamism to a system of metaphoric concepts.[52] They then used this system of concepts to explain how metaphors work. They argued that all actions, events and objects are understood in terms of our experience. The complex relationship of the various aspects of our experience of an action, event or object forms a composite. When we encounter a metaphor, we understand one composite experience in terms of another. Thus, the metaphorical meaning is based upon the projection of one composite experience onto another. What emerges is a new experience that reshapes aspects of our experience, thought and language.

Metaphorical concepts can be further understood in terms of structural metaphors, "physical" metaphors and "orientational" metaphors. Structural metaphors are the most clearly perceived. In structural metaphors, one concept is structured in terms of another concept, eg. **love is food**. This concept, whether we are conscious of it or not, seems to be present in our thoughts, as seen in the common metaphorical expressions such as "bittersweet love", "love is sweet", "love is bitter", "I tasted love", "love is tender", "I devoured her with my eyes", "I have lost my appetite for life", and "I cannot stomach this".

Physical metaphors present events and feelings, or whatever is the subject under discussion, in terms of entities. An example would be a simple statement such as: "My love for antiques is infuriating my family."

"Love for antiques" is a metaphor because the speaker's attitude towards antiques is referred to as an entity that can affect the family.

Another example of a physical metaphor would be: "The brutality of pornography degrades all human beings." The term "brutality of pornography" is a metaphor because pornography is viewed as an entity in order to identify the aspect of it which degrades humanity. The concept of "brutality" is from the physical domain, but is used to structure the concept of being degraded by pornography.

Further examples of physical metaphors include those that view events or ideas as entities in order to quantify them (eg. "There is a lot of anger in this room"), to identify causes (eg. "The pressure of his responsibilities caused his breakdown"), or to set goals or motivate action (eg. "Here's what to do to ensure success in your exams").

While physical metaphors view a concept in terms of entities, orientational metaphors do not really structure one concept in terms of another. Rather, an orientational metaphor organizes a group or system of metaphorical concepts in terms associated with spatial orientation, eg. "up-down" and "front-back". An example would be the fact that so many metaphorical concepts concerning happiness (eg. feeling *up*, spirits were *boosted*, in *high* spirits) have to do with the spatial orientation of **up**, whereas so many metaphorical concepts of unhappiness (eg. feeling *low*, feeling *down*, *sinking* spirits, *falling* into depression) have to do with **down**. Thus, we could say that the orientational metaphor in these statements is **happy is up, sad is down**.

Most of these orientational metaphors seem to suggest that they arise from the physical, social and cultural experiences of a particular group of language users. Perhaps we speak of sad events in terms of **down** because of the drooping physical posture that the human body assumes in times of sadness. This seems plausible, but whether it is definitely the inspiration for such a metaphor is immaterial.

The fact remains that users of the English language have a strong tendency to speak of certain things or events in terms of spatial orientation. This is true to such an extent that it is difficult to imagine talking of certain ideas without the accompanying spatial orientation. For example, we find it almost impossible to speak of good status without resorting to words like "high", which are part of the spatial orientational metaphor **good is up**. In fact, anything to do with the positive (eg. happiness, goodness, high status, good prospects and health) is usually spoken of in terms that suggest height. Negative things, feelings and ideas are expressed in terms that suggest lowness or **down**. Yet, we are not even aware that we are speaking metaphorically when we say something like "I *rose* to the occasion" because this is a conventional way of speaking about that paticular idea or event.

But this is a metaphor nevertheless. These spatial orientational metaphors are so common that we often use them unawares. They even affect other aspects of our speech. For example, in the structural metaphor "love is service", we see the appearance of the spatial orientational metaphor of **good is up** in the expression: "There is no higher love than for a man to give up his life for a friend."

Lakoff's and Johnson's system is based on the idea that we carry understanding in clusters or categories of thought. These clusters are formed from our experiences of life and from our observations and perceptions. The only reason we use these expressions without being consciously metaphorical is that these expressions have become so much a part of everyday use.

Interestingly, in writing of the metaphorical aspect of a particular diagram that depicted human eye responses to a portrait, Danto makes some observations that are equally applicable to rhetorical metaphors and this attribution of qualities to the speaker:

> it is a transfiguration of the portrait in which the portrait... retains its identity through a substitution which is meant to illuminate it under novel attributes: to see that portrait as a diagram is to see that artist as seeing the world as a schematised structure.[53]

Summary The locus of metaphoric expression is in the representation rather than in the reality represented. Metaphor cannot be understood by someone with insufficient knowledge. It is enigmatic or useless to a person without the knowledge of what the expressions represent, and who only has a lexical grasp of the meaning of the words. The metaphorical meaning does not merely lie in the semantic clash but in the new predicative meaning which emerges from the discarding of the literal meaning.

Metaphors can help change the way the listener categorizes and classifies certain aspects of his world and experience. Metaphors that work at the interactive level involve placing known characteristics of the vehicle against those of the tenor to provide new insights about the tenor. Here, a synthesis is created by juxtaposition. This would make it difficult to reduce to literal language. The meaning of the metaphor is thus intuitively grasped. The mind goes through an imaginative leap that is not governed or determined by rules or convention and so is not reducible to a literal paraphrase.

Even the fact that composing a metaphor involves the imagination implies that a metaphor cannot be made completely intelligible by literal language. A metaphor is composed as an original act, like a work of art. Kant refers to this act of originality as genius, the capacity to produce an imaginative representation that "occasions much thought, without however any definite thought, that is, any concept being capable of being adequate to it; it consequently cannot be completely compassed and made intelligible by language."[54]

Metaphors are works of art that offer insights into the imagination and hence cannot be completely or comprehensively restated literally. A critical account of the metaphor in a work of art cannot be a substitute for the work, just as a description of beauty does not activate the same responses as the sight of a beautiful object itself.

How Metaphors Work

Introduction
A taxonomy of theories on metaphors would be almost endless. Many of these theories are abstract and tend to lean toward one of two sides – that metaphor is all important, or that it is of no value, for communication. But theories can help to explain the experience we undergo upon encountering a metaphor. In trying to understand how metaphors work, it helps to consider, at the outset, that there may be two species of metaphor, those that are relatively easy to substitute with a literal expression and those that are not.

Two basic divisions are thus possible; Roman Jakobson distinguished these as metonymy* and metaphor,[55] and Wheelwright distinguished these as epiphor and diaphor.[56] Essentially, both these scholars see two types of metaphorical discourse.

Metonymy or Epiphor
In metonymy or epiphor, the mind compares two experienced objects which can be substituted for one another in myriad ways; it sees similarities in differences, substituting a word for a word, a name for a name. The

metaphorical meaning is carried by a word. It creates "similes, verbal images, verbal icons, parables and myths."[57] Wheelwright's definition of epiphor is "the outreach and extension of meaning through comparison."[58] This type of metaphor depends on juxtaposing experiences to reveal something unexpected yet recognised at once. This is the most common type of metaphorical thinking and usage, and examples abound in statements such as "she is sweeter than sugar" or "he is as grumpy as a bear."

Substitution & Comparison Views

The Substitution and Comparison theories Max Black identified are basically similar to and account for this first type of metaphor[59] – metonymy or epiphor.

The Substitution Theory suggests that the metaphor is an indirect way of saying what could be said literally. This view assumes there is only one meaning that was intended. It is based on the idea that the metaphor is an elliptical simile so that "A is B" is an elliptical form for "A is C". For example, "he is a beanpole" would be an elliptical form for "he is tall."

The Comparison View[60] is a more general version of the Substitution View. Again, it is an indirect way of saying what can be said literally. The speaker is supposed to have an intended literal meaning, a literal set of similarities that fits the context. Thus, "A is B" means "A is like B in being x, y, z" where x, y, z are commonly accepted similarities between A and B that fit the context. In "he is an angel", he is like an angel in being caring and attentive, as angels are assumed to be in folklore.

Haynes calls this comparison rule-governed.[61] Johnson would say the imagination here freely reflects on a series of representations in search of a unifying principle between tenor and vehicle.[62] Similarly, Snell says that some metaphors "may be striking and even witty" but lack the "element of necessity" because they are easily substituted.[63] These tend to be metaphors that rely on a sensory impression of similarity, eg. calling the page of a book a leaf.

Aristotle was of the opinion that all metaphors could be explained by analogical proportionality which, in any comparison, would reveal the *tertium quid comparations*, ie. the quality or aspect of resemblance which makes them "like" or "as" one another. In the proper proportion of the form A:B:C:D, the analogical proportion helps us understand the *explicandum* or meaning. The proportion is symmetrical, as shown by Plato in *Gorgias*.[64] This system of opposables is conveniently self-sufficient, so that if three are known, the fourth can be grasped. The theoretical basis of this view as expressed by Aristotle[65] is that metaphors are elliptical similes so they can be fully understood just by discovering their *tertium quid comparations* or similarity. Aristotle's view here seems to be that any metaphorical statement can be rephrased literally. This would be true if a clear *tertium quid comparations* can always be found as in the case of epiphor or simile that fits within the Comparison Theory. But it would not be the case for diaphoric expressions.

Another difficulty with the Comparison

and Substitution Theories is that they do not explain how the listener knows which similarities to focus on when a speaker uses a metaphor. Also, these theories focus on similarities, ignoring the fact that many metaphors depend on differences to stimulate the listener's imagination to reassess one's usual way of looking at things.

One criticism of the Comparison View is that it does not take into account the fact that even metaphors that do work by similarities tend to focus not on actual qualities of the thing compared, ie. the objective similarity, but on the commonly accepted qualities of the vehicle in that particular culture, ie. subjective similarity. Henle uses the terminology of symbol and icon to try to account for this "double sort of semantic relationship." Symbols signify what is conventionally accepted, and icons signify some similar properties with the tenor. A metaphor works because the symbol in the metaphor provides direction for finding an object or situation. The metaphor implies that "any object or situation fitting the direction may serve as an icon of what one wishes to describe."[66] Notably, the icon is not actually present, but the audience understands what it must be because the iconic element provides a rule for reflecting on what it signifies. This description of how metaphors work has the advantage of taking into account the factors of imagination and insight in understanding a metaphor.

Moreover, metaphors do not always compare two existing things, but can refer to what exists in popular mythology. A common example is the metaphor: "Sally is a dragon." Also, a metaphor need not compare real similarities, but rather what exists in the popular imagination. The metaphorical assertion remains true even though it turns out that the statement of similarity is false. The erroneous insult: "He is a pig" illustrates this. The comparison is meant to be a derogatory comment on someone's hygiene based on the assumption that pigs like mud whereas in fact pigs wallow not for the love of mud but to cool their bodies. Further, there are many metaphors such as: "He has a heart of stone" that do not depend on actual literal similarities.

The Comparison View has the advantage of being simple, of rendering metaphors as simple observations of similarity. The problem with this theory is that it does not account for how all metaphors function as there are metaphors that do not function to draw attention to similarities. Also, the theory does not explain how the mind understands the metaphor or why a metaphor often has the effect of making us feel that a unique moment of insight has taken place, or why it tends to make us restructure our understanding or perception of some aspect of the world.

Metaphor or Diaphor

The second species of metaphor is what Wheelwright calls diaphor and defines as "the creation of new meaning by juxtaposition [through] synthesis."[67] The emphasis is on synthesis, ie. some metaphors bring together different images or experienced objects and make us see what has not before been seen. They present us with a new perspective. We subordinate one way of seeing to another, filter one experience through another and thus create new meaning, and thereby see what could not be seen before. These metaphors would be the more fundamental and "necessary", often not recognized as metaphors at all because of their fundamental function of organizing experience. Wheelwright, Jakobson, Riceour and Max Black emphasize this kind of metaphorical usage that creates similarities, extending meanings rather than introducing new uses of old terms. Snell similarly argues that some metaphors generate a "concept" or offer a conceptual explanation.[68] These metaphorical expressions create resemblances which were not thought of in that way before. These are therefore "necessary" metaphors.

Interaction View

Max Black's Interaction View, based on Richards' opinions, attempts to explain how metaphors are understood without assuming that all metaphoric comprehension depends on the listener recognizing a list of literal, similar properties. His point is that metaphors work not by a comparison of objects for similar properties, but by the interaction of properties that are commonly held to be true of the objects. A metaphor is thus seen as two schemata* of commonplaces that are linked. He describes the process of finding this system of commonplaces or implications as a filtering of the common views of one object through those of another object to produce a new concept or perspective or insight into the subject of the metaphor. This filtering is a thoroughly different activity from comparing objects to pick out resemblances. This filtering makes the metaphor unique so that it cannot be reduced to literal paraphrase.

A weakness in Black's theory is that it is not a universal theory. Black explains the metaphorical process as "a system of associated commonplaces" but this does not explain novel or fresh metaphors as Black himself appears to concede when he says "metaphors can be supported by specifically constructed systems of implications as well as by accepted commonplaces." While saying that these implications usually consist of commonplaces about the subsidiary subject, he points out that they may "in suitable cases, consist of deviant implications established ad hoc by the writer."[69]

Riceour maintains that we cannot make semantic inquiry into how metaphors work if we do not have a psychological theory of how the imagination works with words. The ability of the audience's imagination to enter into the composer's imagination involves some kind of psychological as well as semantic empathy. To complete the semantics of metaphor, Riceour believes we must have recourse to a psychology of imagination.[70] Seeing A as B in a metaphor creates images that produce sense; these images are the concrete representation aroused by the verbal elements and controlled by them. These created images are manifestations of what Riceour calls the "intuitive grasp of a predicative connection."[71] This blurs the distinction between the verbal and nonverbal, or sense and representation.

All this may help explain how a metaphor says what it says. But how do we figure out what a metaphor is about?

Riceour contends that one of the functions of imagination is to give a concrete dimension to the suspension of the ordinary or literal reference. Imagination plays three roles:

1. It schematizes the predicative assimilation between terms by its synthetic insight into similarities;
2. It pictures the sense from the display of images aroused and controlled by the cognitive process; and finally,
3. It contributes concretely to the suspension of ordinary reference and to the projection of new possibilities of redescribing the world by providing models for reading reality in a new way.

Imagination and feeling are genuine components in the Interaction Theory to "achieve the semantic bearing of metaphor."[72] Imagination and feeling do not substitute but complete the cognitive content of metaphor. Riceour acknowledges that his theory is still in its infancy, but it does place due importance on the imagination.

Extending the Interaction Theory, Riceour's work on the theory of imagination as a semantic inquiry provides a way for recognizing the metaphorical purpose of a statement, not based on clues of grammatical and semantic deviance but how it affects, relies on, and plays on the imagination by depicting A as B.

One reason a metaphor works is because the audience willingly suspends the literal lexical system at appropriate moments and engages the imagination to think out what the metaphor is about. In encountering a metaphor, the mind has to find the unstated middle term that connects the vehicle and tenor. If A is metaphorically B, then T is the middle term such that A is to T what T is to B. The middle term has to be determined by the reader as this is the locus of the metaphor; it constitutes the representation of A as B. Of course, this can only be done if the reader is familiar with the attributes that are considered common knowledge about A and B.

Metaphorical Contexts & Intensional* Contexts

Because of the suspension of the ordinary reference of the vehicle in the metaphor, Danto refers to the metaphor as being rendered intensional or unsubstitutable. Thus, metaphors have an intensional structure. Metaphorical words "include among their truth conditions some reference to a representation."[73] Therefore, in "people in glasshouses shouldn't throw stones", the author is not referring to glasshouses or throwing stones but to a constituent of the way the author happens to be representing the act of throwing stones at a glasshouse. This intensional context is thus quite different from what other expressions using words like glass and houses would be about.

Metaphorical contexts are intensional because we cannot substitute them with words which could be used in those other expressions. "Intensional contexts are such because the sentences in whose formations they enter are about specific sentences . . . and not about whatever these sentences or representations would be about were they to occur outside these contexts."[74]

The way metaphor works has much in common with other contexts that are also intensional. One example is the rhetorical use of quotations. As Danto points out, one element of the "metaphoric pragmatics" of the quotation is that the audience is expected to recognize the quotation or allusion.[75] We suggest this is similar to the reader being expected to identify a metaphor because of its incongruent language. A metaphor is effective because of the interaction of ideas about the tenor and vehicle. This is similar to what Danto points out about the quotation, that the reader is expected to recognize the parallels between the situation it is applied to and the original situation of its source. In a metaphor, A is talked of as if it were B. There may be no real similarity to the thing being represented but the locus of the metaphorical expression is in the representation. Similarly, the parallels between a quotation's original, immediate context may not really be there, but are thought to be there. The metaphorical pragmatic exists even if the quotation is not exact and is in fact an unintentional misquote, as long as the audience accepts it as a quotation. Finally, a quote is intensional in the sense that the speaker does not have the choice to substitute any words in the quotation.[76]

The context in which the quote occurs is intensional because the sentence in which it appears is a specific representation, and would not have the same effect in some other sentence or context, or if some other words were used.

A metaphor is intensional because the literal meaning of the vehicle is not what is referred to. In other words, a metaphor or quote does not merely represent subjects. Rather, the mode of representation, i.e. the structure of the metaphor and the use of the quote in a particular sentence, is essential to understanding the metaphor. A word becomes a metaphor when it is used to refer a novel intention and purpose to an aspect of experience so as to disclose an unnamed, different experience. This is basically a reorganizing or refocusing of experience. Something of the same kind happens when a quote is used to create an allusion from a particular known situation to elicit and reveal certain aspects of the immediate context that the audience may not be aware of. This again is a reorganizing and refocusing of the audience's experience or knowledge of the original source of the quote.

Summary

This summary of metaphor's eventful journey in philosophy is by no means exhaustive. It spotlights the high and low points in the reputation of metaphor to make truth claims and to be restated without loss of cognitive content. Opinions on metaphor's epistemological and ontological natures vary according to how one thinks a metaphor works on the human mind. This itself will depend on how one thinks the human mind works. Is the human conceptual system basically metaphorical? Do we encounter, name and think of, and communicate new ideas in terms of what is already known? And do we receive and appropriate new ideas, thoughts and feelings when they are presented in terms of the familiar? If the answer to these is the affirmative, then a definition of metaphor is required that is based on how metaphors work on the imagination.

Method of Analysis of Metaphor in Featured Speeches

In its short history, Singapore has undergone several crises. These include the Communist Threat (1950s), the separation of Singapore from Malaya (August 1965) and the economic recession of 1985–1986. These situations will be described individually, accompanied by transcripts of some speeches that address these topics. The metaphoric analysis then follows.

The method of analysis is basically an application of Lakoff and Johnson's theory that language tends to be structured around certain metaphoric concepts. Each speech will be examined for metaphors and grouped accordingly in clusters or groups where possible. Then the persuasive role that these conceptual metaphors play will be speculated upon. The word "persuasive" is used in its widest sense that all communication is for persuasion, whether the persuasion is done by organising ideas, by presenting ideas in unique ways, or by reminding the audience of existing ideas.

Notes

1. Aristotle, *Rhetoric*, trans. Lane Cooper. (New York: Appleton, 1932), 1405a, 1406b, 1410b, 1412a.
2. Aristotle, *Poetics*, trans. Ingram Bywater. (New York: McGraw-Hill, 1984), 148a, 1457b, 1459a.
3. Aristotle, *Poetics*, 1457b.
4. Aristotle, *Poetics*, 148a.
5. Aristotle, *Poetics*, 1459a.
6. Aristotle, *Rhetoric*, 1406b.
7. Aristotle, *Rhetoric*, 1410b.
8. Aristotle, *Rhetoric*, 1412a.
9. Aristotle, *Rhetoric*, 1405a.
10. Aristotle, *Rhetoric*, 1405a.
11. Aristotle, *Topics*, in *The Works of Aristotle Translated into English*, trans. W.A. Pickard (Oxford: Clarendon Press, 1924), 139b.
12. Cicero, *De Oratore*, trans. H. Rackham (Cambridge: Harvard University Press, 1960), 3.38.156–3.39.157.
13. Quintilian, *Institutio Oratoria*, trans. H. E. Butler (Cambridge: Harvard University Press, 1963), VIII, vi, 8–9.
14. Quintilian, *Institutio Oratoria*, VIII, vi, 2–3.
15. Aristotle, *Poetics*, 1457b.
16. Aristotle, *Poetics*, 1459a.
17. James Edie, *Speaking and Meaning* (Bloomington: Indiana University Press, 1976), 151.
18. Thomas Hobbes, *Leviathan*, ed. C. B. MacPherson (Middlesex: Penguin, 1968), 100–110.
19. Hobbes, *Leviathan*, 116.
20. Hobbes, *Leviathan*, 102.
21. Hobbes, *Leviathan*, 117.
22. John Locke, *Essays Concerning Human Understanding*, ed. A. C. Fraser (New York: Dover, 1959), 34.
23. George Wilhelm Friedrich Hegel, *The Philosophy of Fine Art*, trans. W. M. Bryant (New York: Appleton, 1879), 40–41.

24. John Stuart Mill, *A System of Logic Ratiocinative and Inductive*, ed. J.M. Robson (Toronto: University of Toronto Press, 1974), 800.
25. Edie, 153.
26. Jean-Jacques Rousseau, "Essay on the Origin of Languages," in *On the Origin of Language*, trans. J. H. Moran (New York: Frederick Ungar, 1966), 12–13.
27. Frederick Nietzsche, "On Truth and Falsity in Their Ultramoral Sense," in *The Complete Works of Frederick Nietzsche*, trans. Maxilian A. Magge, ed. Oscar Levy (New York: Gordon Press, 1974), 180.
28. Nietzsche, 180.
29. Nietzsche, 180.
30. C. K. Ogden and I. A. Richards, *The Meaning of Meaning* (New York: Harcourt, Brace and Co., 1946), 149.
31. Edie, 169.
32. I. A. Richards, *The Philosophy of Rhetoric* (Oxford: Oxford University Press, 1936).
33. Max Black, "Metaphor," in *Models and Metaphor: Studies in Language and Philosophy* (Ithaca: Cornell University Press, 1962), 25–47.
34. Richards, 92.
35. Hobbes, *Leviathan*, 116–117.
36. Richards, 108.
37. Richards, 108–109.
38. Nelson Goodman, *Languages of Art* (Indianapolis: Bobbs-Merrill, 1968), 71.
39. Richards, 93.
40. Arthur Danto, *The Transfiguration of the Commonplace* (Cambridge: Harvard University Press, 1981), 176.
41. Monroe Beardsley, "The Metaphorical Twist," *Philosophy and Phenomelogical Research*, 22 (1962): 293–307.
42. Paul Henle, "Metaphor," in *Language, Thought and Culture*, ed. Paul Henle (Ann Arbor: University of Michigan Press, 1958), 183.
43. Goodman, 69.
44. Ina Loewnberg, "Identifying Metaphors," *Foundations of Language* 12 (1975): 331.
45. Max Black, "More About Metaphor," in *Metaphor and Thought*, ed. Andrew Ortony (Cambridge: Cambridge University Press, 1979), 36.
46. Black, "More About Metaphor", 36.

47. Mark Johnson, "Introduction: Metaphor in the Philosophical Tradition," in *Philosophical Perspectives on Metaphor*, ed. Mark Johnson (Minneapolis: University of Minnesota Press, 1981), 23.
48. Paul Riceour, "The Metaphorical Process as Cognition, Imagination and Feeling," *Critical Inquiry* 5 (1978): 145–146.
49. Riceour, 146.
50. Edwin Black, "The Second Persona," *Quarterly Journal of Speech* (April 1970): 109–119.
51. Edie, 152.
52. George Lakoff and Mark Johnson, "Conceptual Metaphor in Everyday Language," in *Metaphors We Live By* (Chicago: University of Chicago Press, 1980), 286–325.
53. Danto, 172.
54. Immanuel Kant, *Critique of Judgement*, trans. J. H. Bernard (New York: Hafner Press, 1951), 157.
55. Roman Jakobson, *Essais de linguistique generale* (Paris: Minuit, 1963), 61.
56. Philip Wheelwright, *Metaphor and Reality* (Bloomington: University of Indiana Press, 1962), 72.
57. Edie, 190.
58. Wheelwright, 72.
59. Black, "Metaphor", 25–47.
60. Henle, 173–195.
61. Haynes, Felicity, "Metaphor as Interactive," *Educational Theory* 25 (1975), 273.
62. Johnson, 39.
63. Bruno Snell, *The Discovery of the Mind* (New York: Harper, 1960), 198.
64. For example, Plato's comparison of rhetoric to philosophy and its relationship to cookery as it compares to medicine. See Plato, *Gorgias*, trans. W. C. Helmbold (New York: Bobbs-Merrill, 1952), 100ff.
65. Aristotle, *Rhetoric*, 1406b.
66. Henle, 178.
67. Wheelwright, 72.
68. Snell, 205.
69. Black, "Metaphor", 43–44.
70. Riceour, 143.
71. Riceour, 151.

72. Riceour, 154–155.
73. Danto, 181.
74. Danto, 187.
75. Danto, 182.
76. Danto, 183–184.

Glossary of Technical Terms

basic semantic unit – "semantic" refers to meaning in language. A semantic unit is an item in language that conveys meaning or a definite idea. It doesn't need to be a whole word, may even be part of a word, eg. the basic semantic unit for "going" is "go".

deviant denomination – the act of naming something with other than its usual common name.

intensional – describes the sum of attributes contained in a concept or implied by a term. It describes a word or statement that has no substitute to convey the particular meaning that it does in a particular context.

lexical deviance – "lexical" refers to the dictionary definition. A lexical deviance occurs when a word is used to mean something other than its dictionary definition.

metonymy – a figure of speech characterized by the use of the name of one thing in place of the name of something that it symbolizes, eg. crown for king.

paradigmatic – a term used in linguistic circles to describe the relationship operating between an element at a given level and the elements of a sentence, eg. the relationship between a word and its function in a sentence.

deviant predication – occurs when a word is applied to suggest an unexpected attribute or quality about something.

schemata – a schema is a kind of standard which the mind forms from past experiences and by which new experiences can be evaluated.

tenor/vehicle – The tenor is the subject to which the metaphoric word is applied. The vehicle is the metaphoric word or word cluster. For example, "My love (tenor) is like a red, red rose (vehicle)."

trope – a general term for a figure of speech/ thought.

2. The Communist Threat (Middle To Late 1950s)

Historical Background

Spanning different periods, the Communist Threat was represented by the Hock Lee riots, the ideological offerings of the Chinese middle schools, the pursuit of a Communist Malaya and the attempted Communist infiltration into the People's Action Party (PAP).

Briefly, we shall look at two incidents:

1. The Communist infiltration of the PAP in 1957, and
2. A showdown initiated by the "PLEN" of the Communist Party.

One of the Communists' most threatening move was a calculated attempt to infiltrate the PAP. The leftist force was led by Lim Chin Siong. With several other members, Lim Chin Siong made the Communist presence felt in the Central Executive Committee (CEC) of the PAP. In the August 1957 annual meeting of the PAP, an important resolution was made to add the term "non-Communist" to the party's manifesto. The resolution was adopted. At this meeting, Lee Kuan Yew pointed out that it was the PAP's objective to create a socialist society. In this, the PAP objective coincided with the Communist objective. Only the approach in attaining a socialist society was different. Unlike the Communists, whose ideology was characterized by dictatorial leadership, the PAP preferred a democratic, socialist style of government.

Lee Kuan Yew was wary of Communist infiltration and was anxious lest a split occur in the PAP. The danger was imminent as the elections had put an equal number of Communists and non-Communists in the CEC. Fearing public perception of the CEC as a Communist front, and being apprehensive that the non-Communists in the CEC would be unwittingly used to advance Communist ideology, Lee Kuan Yew and the other non-Communist members of the CEC refused to assume office. Lee Kuan Yew announced that since there was no majority of a non-Communist group, he would not want to assume the right to lead the party. This was a well-calculated move to avoid being associated with the Communist members as well as to avoid compromising the ideology of the non-Communist group.

Coerced to assume leadership, the Communists did so against their own wishes. Normally, a typical Communist strategy would be to work behind the scenes, using non-Communists to stage a false front. However, the Communist-led CEC did not last long. In a mass arrest of pro-Communists by the Labour Front government, all except one of the CEC members were detained. The one who was not arrested, T. T. Rajah, resigned from the CEC.

It is unclear whether the move by the Labour Front government to arrest and detain the Communists was a direct response to halt the threat of the non-Communists in the CEC. But it was timely for Lee Kuan Yew and the other ex-CEC leaders because it set the stage for the PAP victory in the general elections in 1959.

Despite the PAP's resounding victory in the elections, the Communists remained undeterred. In 1958, as their representative to the PAP, the Communists used Fang Chuan Pi (Lee refers to him as the PLEN, as in Plenipotentiary, in the speech that follows). Fang tried to persuade Lee to collaborate by advancing an anti-colonial front but Lee did not agree to collaboration with the Communists. Apparently, however, Fang's strategy did not just include persuading Lee. He also had his designs on the Minister for National Development, Ong Eng Guan. Ong had been deemed ineffective and unable to discharge his duties and Lee had taken over his portfolio. In response, Ong had criticised the PAP for being undemocratic and resigned with two other PAP members to head the United People's Front.

The Hong Lim seat vacated by Ong was contested in a by-election in April 1961. Ong Eng Guan won a resounding victory. Across the causeway, Tunku Abdul Rahman expressed anxiety over this, fearing that Singapore would be taken over by the Communists and used as a base to later spread Communism in Malaya. Malaya was therefore indirectly threatened. The Tunku then alluded to the possibility of a merger. This was good news to Lee because merger would ensure that the anti-Communist Malayan Government would thwart Communist activity. In retaliation, the Communists attacked the PAP by declaring that it was undemocratic. This led to the crossing over of several members of the PAP to the Communist camp. The Communists even supported David Marshall from the Workers' Party. Backed by the Communists, Marshall won the Anson seat which became available after the death of PAP's assemblyman for Anson. Marshall demanded Lee's resignation. Lee later wrote to the CEC and left his premiership to the decision of the CEC. However, the chairman of the CEC, Toh Chin Chye, maintained his confidence in Lee, a vote of confidence that was endorsed by the CEC. Lee declared that the Communist Left and the British Government had designed to overthrow the PAP. Even though a vote of confidence for Lee was maintained, a series of resignations and cross-overs resulted in an uneven voting position for the PAP in the Assembly. The PAP however held on to this precarious position. Among the wisest moves at that time was to avoid holding by-elections so that the majority vote did not belong to the Communists.

Much more can be said about Communism in Singapore (the massive strikes, boycotts, demonstrations, riots, etc.), but for the purpose of speech analysis, a brief outline of the volatile nature of the Communists is sufficient. Equally potent was Lee's rhetoric.

We shall now analyse the extent to which metaphor played a role in two of Lee's speeches.

"How The Communists Operate"

Speech

This speech, delivered on 18 August 1961 by Lee Kuan Yew, is one in a series of broadcast talks aired over Radio Singapore from 13 September to 9 October 1961.

Source: *The Battle For Merger* (Singapore: Government Printing Office, 1962).

This talk is largely a personal narrative. It will explain how I came to know the Communists, what they are after in Malaya, who they are, how they operate, why we worked on parallel line with them for many years and why eventually we have parted company over merger.

Let me take my story back to 1950 when I began to learn the realities of political life in Malaya. At that time every genuine nationalist who hated the British colonial system wanted freedom and independence. That was a time when only weak men and stooges came out and performed on the local political stage. Fierce men were silent or had gone underground to join the Communists.

There were the Progressive Party and their feeble leaders. There were the clowns of the Labour Party of Singapore. When I met acquaintances like Lim Kean Chye and John Eber and asked them what they were doing, why they were allowing these things to go on, they smiled and said, "Ah well! What can be done in such a situation?"

One morning in January 1951, I woke up and read in the newspapers that John Eber had been arrested, that Lim Kean Chye had disappeared and escaped arrest. Shortly afterwards a reward was offered for his arrest. Politics in Malaya was a deadly serious business. These are not clowns or jokers. They had decided to go with the Communists.

So my colleagues and I pressed on working with the unions. The only unions able to take fierce and militant action were those with no Communist affiliations whatsoever. The postmen went on strike. I acted for them. We extracted every ounce of political and material advantage out of the dispute with the colonial government and got them maximum benefits.

The Post and Telegraph workers wanted their salaries to be revised and backdated. The dispute went to arbitration. We helped them and exposed the stupidities and inadequacies of the colonial administration. The whole of the government civil service was organized to revolt against non-pensionable expatriation pay for the benefit of a few white men.

You remember my colleagues, Dr. Goh Keng Swee and K.M. Byrne, organized a fight against the European half of the civil service. So we went on organizing the workers in their unions, rallying them to fight the British colonial system for freedom, for a more just and equal society.

Meanwhile, I had got in touch with the people who were detained in the same batch as John Eber. They were the English-educated group of the Anti-British League, a Communist organization. The ABL relation to the MCP is like that of the volunteer force to the regular professional army.

I was instructed to act for one of them. I came to know and liked him. Subsequently in 1953 he was released from detention. We became friends. He told me that he was a Communist. I will call him Laniaz. He is still a most important Communist cadre spreading propaganda on behalf of the Communist cause.

Through him I came to know Devan Nair, who was the most determined ABL member I have ever known. Subsequently, I discovered that Devan Nair was in fact on the way to being a full-fledged Communist Party member.

We became comrades in the united front in the unions and in the PAP. Devan Nair knew I was not a Communist; he knew that I knew he was a Communist. In 1956 he landed in jail together with Lim Chin Siong and company.

After spending a great part of his life with the Malayan Communist Party, he came to his own conclusion that their leadership was inadequate to meet the needs of the revolution in Malaya.

Determined and dedicated though they were, they had their shortcomings and were unable to make the necessary changes in policy and approach, to create a national based movement for their Communist cause.

Devan Nair is now on our side. On the other hand, S.T. Bani, Assemblyman for Thomson, who was not a Communist and who had for several years worked together with me in the unions competing against the Communists, decided some time last year to throw in his lot with the Communists. He had been won over to their side. So the battle goes on for the hearts and minds, first of the political elite of the population, and ultimately of the whole population.

Laniaz joined us, a core of English-educated, to fight colonialism. We were all non-Communists other than Laniaz – Dr. Toh, Dr. Goh, K.M. Byrne, Rajaratnam and myself. We organized and worked in the unions, recruited cadres of our own in the English-educated and Malay-educated world. We drew up plans for the setting up of the party.

Riots

Then one day in 1954 we came into contact with the Chinese-educated world. The Chinese middle school students were in revolt against national service and they were beaten down. Riots took place, charges were preferred in court. Through devious ways they came into contact with us.

We bridged the gap to the Chinese-educated world – a world teeming with vitality, dynamism and revolu-

tion, a world in which the Communists had been working for over the last thirty years with considerable success.

We the English-educated revolutionaries went in trying to tap this oil-field of political resources, and soon found our pipelines crossing those of the Communist Party. We were latecomers trying to tap the same oil-fields. We were considered by the Communists as poaching in their exclusive territory.

In this world we came to know Lim Chin Siong and Fong Swee Chuan. They joined us in the PAP. In 1955 we contested the elections. Our initiation into the intricacies and ramifications of the Communist underground organization in the trade unions and cultural associations had begun.

The Underground

It is a strange business working in this world. When you meet a union leader you will quickly have to decide which side he is on and whether or not he is a Communist. You can find out by the language he uses, and his behaviour, whether or not he is in the inner circle which makes the decisions. These are things from which you determine whether he is an outsider or an insider in the Communist underworld.

I came to know dozens of them. They are not crooks or opportunists. These are men with great resolve, dedicated to the Communist revolution and to the establishment of the Communist state believing that it is the best thing in the world for mankind.

Many of them are prepared to pay the price for the Communist cause in terms of personal freedom and sacrifice. They know they run the risk of detention if they are found out and caught. Often my colleagues and I disagreed with them, and intense fights took place, all concealed from the outside world because they were Communists working in one united anti-colonial front with us against the common enemy, and it would not do to betray them.

Eventually many of them landed in jail, in the purges in 1956 and 1957. I used to see them there, arguing their appeals, reading their captured documents and the Special Branch precis of the cases against them.

I had the singular advantage of not only knowing them well by having worked at close quarters with them in a united front against the British, but I also saw the official version in reports on them.

Many were banished to China. Some were my personal friends. They knew that I knew they were Communists, for between us there was no pretence. They believed that I should join them. They believed that ultimately I would be forced to admit that what they call the "bourgeois" democratic system could not produce a just and equal society, and that I would admit that they were right.

On the other hand, I used to spend hours arguing with some of them trying to prove to them that whatever else happened to China or Russia, we were living in Malaya and, irrespective of Communism or democratic socialism, if we wanted to build a more just and equal society in Malaya, we would have to make certain fundamental decisions, such as being Malayans, uniting the Chinese and Indians and others with the Malays, building up national unity and national loyalty, and rallying all the races together through a national language.

MCP Strength

Lim Chin Siong is not the beginning nor the end of Communism. He is only one of their disciplined open-front workers. When the Emergency started in 1948, he was only a young boy about 15 or 16 years old in the Chinese High School.

The strength of the MCP lies in the propagation of Communist theories and ideals to recruit able and idealistic young men and women to join them in their cause. Our able young men on their side can by working in a union, fighting for better pay and conditions of service for workers, get thousands of workers on to their side.

Let me explain this. In 1953 I became legal adviser to the Naval Base Labour Union, fought their case and won the confidence of the committee and the men. They were looking for a union secretary. I introduced to them S. Woodhull, a person I had then known in the University of Malaya Socialist Club for one-and-a-half years.

I knew that he was anti-British and anti-colonial. I also knew he was reading Marxism and that he was initiating himself into the mysteries of world revolution. But he was not a Communist or a member of the ABL although they were grooming him for recruitment. He was then prepared to work for a cause. On my recommendation he became secretary to the union.

He worked hard and by 1955, two years afterwards, he had organized with the help of a handful of dedicated non-Communist activists like Ahmad Ibrahim and a few Communist ground workers in the union, 7,500 workers in the Base.

He had organized them into a coherent force which would listen to him, not because the workers believed in socialism or Communism, but because the workers knew him to be a trustworthy and industrious man who worked with me for them.

In this way, the Communists, although they had only a few hundred active cadres, could muster and rally thousands of people in the unions, cultural organizations and student societies.

By working and manifestly appearing to work selflessly, and ceaselessly, they won the confidence and regard of the people in the organizations. Having won the confidence and regard, they then got the people to support their political stand.

The strength of the Communist Party lies not in their mass as such but in the band of trained and disciplined cadres, who lead the masses into the Communist causes, often without the masses knowing they are Communists.

The Communist Threat 49

Metaphoric Analysis

This speech was part of a series of talks called "Battle for Merger" broadcast over Radio Singapore on 18 September 1961. The audience consisted of people who most likely had been around during the 50s, the period to which the speech alludes, as well as those who had since attained an interest in Singapore's past.

Attempting a metaphoric criticism of Lee Kuan Yew's speeches is not an easy task as some words or phrases in fact do not qualify as traditional or conventional metaphors, but contain metaphoric pragmatics and thus qualify as metaphor, by our definition. Analysis of these metaphors enlightens one about how metaphors persuade.

A metaphoric analysis of this speech becomes complicated when we consider its rhetorical style. Lee's style here consists of personal narratives. Narratives recount past events and seldom rely heavily on metaphors. Sometimes narratives do employ metaphors, but how they fit into an overall metaphoric concept is more complicated. Nevertheless, they function metaphorically even if they do not contain conventional metaphors.

This speech recalls that in retaliation against the rule of British colonialism, many locals had entered the political stage by entering or organising local political parties. Some had joined the Communists. Lee describes the former as "jokers", "clowns" and "crooks". In contrast, the latter are described as a more serious-minded people. In the middle of the speech, Lee says that the Communists are "men with great resolve, dedicated to the Communist revolution." They are not "crooks".

The metaphoric concept governing the metaphors "jokers", "clowns" and "crooks" is the structural metaphor:

Communists are serious-minded people.

The metaphors "jokers", "clowns" and "crooks" describe the Communists in terms of who or what they are not. The audience is supposed to perceive the denotations and connotations of the metaphors. They are then to go one step further and decipher which aspects or characteristics of these metaphors are used in direct opposition to the Communists and which are not.

"Joker" generally has three definitions:

1. one who tells or plays jokes;
2. a playing card, used in certain games as the highest ranking card or as a wild card; and
3. a minor clause in a document such as a legislative bill that voids or changes its original or intended purpose.

These denotative meanings (dictionary definitions) of "joker" do not appear sufficient to describe what the Communists are not. Instead, Lee calls for a connotative (a community's jargon or definition) meaning. A joker connotes characteristics such as playfulness, mischievousness and buffoonery. Lee says that the Communists exist not to provoke amusement and mischief. Rather, they are serious-minded people.

Similarly, the Communists are not "clowns". They are not in the business of providing laughter or jesting. Interestingly, the word "clown" denotes a "coarse, rude person." This strongly suggests to the audience that the Communists are perhaps polite, well-mannered, civil and courteous.

Even though the statement: "Communists are not crooks" is ideologically debatable, Lee's use of "crooks" here points to the method in which the Communists operate. The implication is that these "crooks" are not fraudulent, corrupt or dishonest. They do not have the intention to cheat. The implication is that the Communists are a serious-minded group and that they sincerely believe that the Communist manifesto benefits all of humankind.

Lee differentiates between the political activists of the 50s, namely, "clowns", "jokers" and "fierce men". The "clowns" and "jokers" are further described as "weak men" and "stooges". This distinction is useful as it takes advantage of the prevailing perception of the local politicians of the decade before this speech was made. This view of the politicians is encapsulated in the metaphor of performers on a stage. The metaphor covers the image of "clown", "joker" and "stooge" and recalls a gestalt that includes entertainment, frivolity and buffoonery. The listener is reminded that his own view of the politicians dictated that they cannot be taken seriously as their ideas were considered trivial and paltry. If a listener does not immediately recall the political scene of the 50s, or even if a listener did not have an opinion of the politics of the time, the terms "clowns" and "jokers" immediately conjure a picture and create the whole mood of the times. This saves the speaker and the listener the trouble of going into great detail about something that is not the main subject of the speech.

The metaphors "jokers", "clowns" and "crooks" are used in negation ("they are not..."), demanding the audience to sift out denotation from connotation and connotation from denotation. The universal understanding (denotation) of these words would not convey the derision and dismissive tone that is evoked by the connotative meaning of the terms, as would be immediately assigned by the local listening audience. In this sense, these words function metaphorically for the audience who would immediately recognise a situation where a speaker refers to politician "A" in terms of "B", ie. "clown", "crook" and "joker".

Metaphor by negation demands that the audience take an extra step cognitively. Unlike a regular metaphor such as: "He is a dragon", a metaphor by negation (ie. "He is not a dragon") insists on the extra step of sensing what is the appropriate opposite. This operation asserts another sifting out of what might be termed "antonymic expressions", whereby the audience has to look at the implied opposite of a common term or phrase. In other words, the audience has to figure out for itself what it means to be the opposite of "jokers", "clowns" and "crooks". The gestalt of not being "clowns" and jokers" is guided by the term "fierce men". The term "Communists" therefore creates a complex of ideas that includes "deadly serious" and "earnest". Thus, the use of the terms "fierce men" and "Communists" guides the listener to infer that those who are not "jokers", "clowns" and "crooks" are deadly serious, earnest and dangerous.

A question can be asked about the efficacy of using a metaphor by negation. It seems that the goal of this speech is not to embark on a comprehensive ideological description of the Communists. Rather, it is to capture the "face" of the Communist in a quick, thumbnail sketch. Details would only distract.

Metaphor by negation in this context is effective since the objective of the speech is singular. Metaphor by negation takes a little more time for the audience to figure out and this opportunity for deliberation seems purposeful. The brevity of the speech emphasizes its singular purpose, ie. to determine the characteristics of the Communist.

Another metaphor that recurs in the speech is that of conflict. This is conveyed by terms associated with war, such as "fierce men", "feeble leaders", "gone underground", "fierce and militant action", "cadre", "revolution", "united front", "rallying", "loyalty", "open front", "recruit", "recruitment", "fighting" (for better pay), "fought their case", "muster and rally", "strength" and "band of trained and disciplined cadres". Together, these terms form a structural metaphor, thus evoking the concept:

The communists are warriors.

The impact of this metaphorical concept is the message that the Communists are not to be taken lightly. They are determined to win. Part of the gestalt of the metaphor of warrior is "enemy". Thus, the audience will immediately identify the Communists as the enemy. Another element of the gestalt of the metaphor of warrior is "territory" or "land in dispute". Thus, the audience will make the connection that the Communists in fact wanted Singapore for themselves. This is reinforced by the statement: "by working and manifestly appearing to work selflessly and ceaselessly", which conveys the idea that while seemingly working for others, the enemy was in fact secretly working to get Singapore for itself.

Summary of Analysis	Extending the definition of metaphor to the narrative style helps us to further understand why this speech is persuasive. The style of the whole speech is narrative, and the aim of narrative is to transport the audience to another place and time. In this sense, the metaphoric pragmatic is to make the audience see the situation in the speech as if it were currently happening, so that the audience will view the situation in a particular light, certainly in the light that these events required a firm response. In effect, the sense of being transported to the past serves to

convince the audience that if they had been in that situation, they would have had to make similar choices. Thus, if to appreciate the metaphor is to see A in terms of B, then the metaphoric pragmatic of the narrative style in the speech can be simply put as "see yourselves as if you were the key figures in this narrative". By seeing A in terms of B, the audience is persuaded to accept the speaker's views as he facilitates their understanding and appreciation of past events.

"Envoy From The Underground"

Speech

This speech, delivered on 22 September 1961 by Lee Kuan Yew, is one in a series of broadcast talks aired over Radio Singapore from 13 September to 9 October 1961.

Source: *The Battle For Merger* (Singapore: Government Printing Office, 1962).

There may be people who say that all this talk of the Communist underground is a fairy tale. I shall have to tell you something which is known to very few people.

In March 1958, before I went with the All-Party Merdeka Mission to the London talks, someone whom I knew to be connected with the Communist organization approached me and arranged for me to see a man who he said would like to see me and discuss some matters.

I met him in Singapore one afternoon on the road between Victoria Memorial Hall and the Legislative Assembly and took him to a room in the Legislative Assembly. He was a Chinese-educated young man several years younger than myself – an able and determined person.

He told me that he was a representative of the Communist Party in Singapore. I told him that I did not know who he was and I had no way of knowing the truth of his claim. He explained that his purpose in seeing me was to establish cooperation between the Communists and the non-Communists in the PAP.

You will remember that the Communists had been purged in 1956 and 1957. Some of them had given trouble to the PAP. He told me that they were all young and enthusiastic people who did not understand the Communist policy of the united front, but that they meant well and wanted to help bring about the Communist revolution in Malaya.

He wanted to re-establish cooperation in the united anti-colonial front with the PAP. I shall call him the PLEN, short for plenipotentiary. We spoke in Chinese. Sometimes I used English words to clarify my meaning and I found that he understood English.

I asked him for proof to show me that he was a genuine representative of the MCP. He smiled and said that I had to take his word for it. I then asked him whether he had authority over the open-front Communist cadres in the unions and political parties, and I gave as an example Chang Yuen Tong.

Chang was then a City Councillor and Executive Committee member of the Workers Party. He is now the President of the Electrical and Wireless Employees Union and is on the protem committee of the new Communist trade union united front, SATU.

I knew he was one of the pro-Communist trade union workers, I told the PLEN that I thought the Communists were trying to make use of David Marshall's Workers Party to fight the PAP. They had used the Workers Party to fight us in the Jalan Besar Division in the City Council elections and they had lost on a close fight.

I said that as evidence of his credentials that he was a real representative of the Communist Command in Singapore and his good faith in not wishing to attack the PAP by using the Workers Party as an instrument, he should give the word for the resignation of Chang

The Communist Threat 57

Yuen Tong from the Workers Party and the City Council and let the Workers Party and David Marshall go on their own. He said, "All right. Give us some time. We shall see that it is done."

Several weeks later in April 1958 while I was in London for the constitutional talks, I read in the newspapers that Chang Yuen Tong had resigned from the Workers Party and from the City Council. The MCP had given orders. THE PLEN had proved his credentials.

Communist Aid Withdrawn

Subsequently, in the City Council by-election at Kallang, David Marshall, without Communist support, and after all the foolish policies of his party in the City Council, found himself with just over one hundred votes at the end of a campaign in which he was most times talking to empty fields. The Communists had withdrawn support and the Workers Party collapsed.

When the Workers Party was formed hurriedly in November 1957, they were able to win three out of the four seats they contested in the City Council elections in December 1957. They did this with the help of the Communist supporters who had broken with PAP after the 1957 conflict in the PAP and the purge which took place.

Only one Workers Party candidate lost and that was to a PAP candidate, Chan Chee Seng, in the Jalan Besar Division. But in the last general elections in 1959, the Communist supporters had abandoned the Workers Party and everyone of their candidates lost.

Before the general elections in 1959, I met the PLEN altogether on four occasions, all in Singapore, each time at a different rendezvous. We discussed things generally. He was trying to gauge the PAP's intentions and purpose. He wanted again and again to find out if we were prepared to let the Communists work together with us in a united anti-colonial front in the PAP.

I told him that I did not see much virtue in this, because from time to time we were going to have repetitions of the troubles we had in 1956 and 1957. Each time the

MCP decided to take a different line, we the PAP would be involved. I told him it was far better from the PAP point of view that the Communists left us alone.

They had their other open-front organizations. They could work on parallel lines if they chose to, but if they decided to change policy they could please themselves – it would not damage the PAP. He tried to allay my doubts. He said that Lim Chin Siong and the others I had dealt with may have given me an unfortunate impression as a result of my unhappy experiences in 1956 and 1957. But this time I was dealing with the top, the men who decided and gave the orders, and they would keep their word.

He said Lim could not decide policy and the errors were made because of the difficulty of communicating instructions to him in time. I did not commit myself to anything in reply. Never in any one of our meetings did I say or do anything which would commit the PAP. We left things at that. The general elections came in May 1959. But I was to meet him again in May this year.

MCP Supports Party Rakyat

In 1959, it was quite clear to everybody, including the Communists, that the PAP was in for a landslide victory. Because of the corruption and stupidities of the people then in power, we were the obvious choice for the people. The PAP therefore fielded 51 candidates to cover all 51 constituencies.

The MCP supporters fought us through the Party Rakyat only in four constituencies – Aljunied, Kampung Kembangan, Geylang Serai and Siglap. It was difficult for them to work up enthusiasm against the PAP and as the election campaign went on the amount of effort put in for the Party Rakyat by the Communist cadres and their supporters in their unions flagged away. As a result, the Party Rakyat was defeated in all four constituencies.

In all the other areas where there were no Party Rakyat candidates, the MCP was neutral and at best their supporters may have voted for the PAP.

But we never asked for their support. Even during the election campaign you will remember that we made our non-Communist stand quite clear. In several speeches, I stressed the distinction between us and the Communists. I posed the problems that we would face after we won the elections.

Let me quote from one of my election rally speeches made at Clifford Pier on May 26, 1959, published in the *Straits Times*, *Nanyang Siang Pau* and *Sin Chew Jit Poh*. I stated that the real fight would begin after the general elections in which the ultimate contestants would be the PAP and the MCP. This would be the fight to establish the democratic system in the hearts and minds of the people. I said:

> In this fight, the ultimate contestants will be the PAP and the MCP – the PAP for a democratic, non-Communist, socialist Malaya, and the MCP for a Soviet Republic of Malaya. It is a battle that cannot be won by just bayonets and bullets. It is a battle of ideals and ideas. And the side that recruits more ability and talent will be the side that wins.

I further said that PAP would not adopt the behaviour of David Marshall or that of Lim Yew Hock in combating the Communists, because Marshall was vacillating, pushed from pillar to post and retreating in the face of each demonstration and because Tun Lim Yew Hock only used the big "stick and gun" as his answer till finally the GOC Singapore Base District and his helicopters took over. The PAP would not fall into either of these errors.

This was all said nearly two-and-a-half years ago during the last general elections. We knew all along what we had to expect. It was no smear then. It is not a smear now.

In my next talk I shall tell you how after I met the PLEN again in May this year, the Communists and the nationalists came to the parting of ways.

Metaphoric Analysis

This speech was given four days after "How the Communists Operate". Both speeches were part of a series delivered over Radio Singapore. "Envoy From the Underground" focusses on the action of one man, whom Lee calls the "PLEN". The word "underground" immediately links this speech with the warrior metaphor in the previous speech and thus identifies the envoy as a representative of the enemy.

Lee points out that the "PLEN" is short for plenipotentiary. Here, we see a distinct example of the speaker wanting the audience to see A as B. In using the "PLEN" as a metaphor, Lee wants the audience to see the plenipotentiary as some figure without a human name, identified by an abbreviated designation. A plenipotentiary is one who is vested with full powers and functions of an ambassador or an envoy. Lee indicates that such is the function of the "PLEN".

The "PLEN" has been vested with full powers of an ambassador of the Communists. The power is manifested in his ability to cause Chang Yuen Tong to resign from the Workers' Party and from the City Council. Lee said after Chang stepped down: "The "PLEN" had proved his credentials." This proved that the existence of the Communist underground was not a "fairy tale". At the end of the account of how the "PLEN" proved his credentials, the reader will inevitably recall that the account began with that assertion. The term "fairy tale" acts as a metaphor, recalling a gestalt of ideas to do with the concept of "fairy tale", eg. harmless, childish, fantasy, make-believe, distortion and diversion. It also causes the audience to associate with the Communist Party the concept that the underground is "not a fairy tale". Here again is a metaphor that works by negation or antonymic expression. The complex of ideas would probably include dangerous, real and harmful. The reference to the Communist underground evokes not only the idea of warfare. The audience is also free to associate it with other concepts such as "secret", "sinister" and perhaps even "deadly".

The metaphoric pragmatic of referring to the "PLEN" as one who is vested with full powers underscores the power of naming. He could have been named the "crafty one" or the "trickster" or the "chameleon" but none of these was adequate to describe the ambassadorial status and power assumed by the "PLEN". The "PLEN" thus becomes an appropriate metaphor to describe the man who was "a genuine representative of the MCP".

Interestingly, the article "the" prefaces "PLEN". This implies that there is one "PLEN". He is the one and only. The article "the" thus emphasizes the "PLEN's" imputed power and his special status among the Communists in Singapore.

Doubtless, there is something diminutive about shortening a person's name, let alone shortening a term that is used to refer to a person. For example, when one is called "Johnny" (for "Jonathan") or "Seng" (for "Hock Seng") or "Bill" (for "William"), the shorter version smacks of a robbing of formality or even importance. It is not necessarily an insult, but it definitely takes away the official dignity of the original form. Lee recognizes that a plenipotentiary is synonymous with an "envoy" or an "ambassador", one who is surely to be accorded respect and treated with dignity. So, he uses the diminutive "PLEN" because he wants the audience to realize that this is a representative of deceit and duplicity, rather than a dignified envoy. Thus, the audience would not accord him the same respect as they would any other ambassador.

Even if the actual name of the "PLEN" was known at that time and communicated to the audience, using it would remove the element of mystery which the term the "PLEN" evokes. This absence of a human name and the shortening of the title make the term the "PLEN" mysterious, sinister and secretive. Indeed, many titles, eg. "king", while distancing the human element, enlarge the element of respectful dignity. But the "PLEN" reduces the element of respect and homage. Little wonder then Lee calls him the "PLEN". On the other hand, because the "PLEN" has such wide-reaching powers as to alter the political horizon of the country, the term becomes a metaphor for the sinister, the secret, the powerful, the undignified and the fearful.

The metaphor the "PLEN" shrouds the person in complete secrecy and mystery. The use of this metaphor and its associations with the Communist Party prevents the audience from becoming comfortably familiar with his real name. For example, if the envoy's name were similar to a family member's name, it might evoke empathy, or even a racial or traditional empathy. It is imperative that the audience recognize this person as an envoy from the Communist Party, and not an ordinary man with an ordinary name, like any other person. The speaker wants the audience to be aware that the "PLEN" is a holder of power and status in the Communist Party.

In recounting his encounters with this secret force the "PLEN", the speaker proves to the audience that he is a worthy leader of the nation. The speech in effect lists the ways in which the speaker first tested and then handled an adversary as powerful as the "PLEN". This test of the "PLEN's" linguistic ability and his level of power in the Communist Party serves two functions. It shows the power of the "PLEN", and at the same time points to the wisdom of the speaker in defending the nation from the forces of the "PLEN".

This speech is brief and there is an absence of easily identifiable metaphors. The title the "PLEN" carries an emotive and highly-charged metaphoric pragmatic, which the speaker correctly uses to portray the character of the person and of the organization he represents. The metaphor also carries more metaphoric import than an easily identifiable or traditional metaphor (eg. "he is a chameleon"), by virtue of the diminution of the title and the sinister mystery that the unusual nickname evokes. At the same time, the audience is assured that they have a fine, upright and intelligent leader to protect the nation.

The duality created, ie. the "PLEN" vs. the speaker, suggests a metaphor of conflict, competition, perhaps even war, where the audience realizes that a "battle" was waged for the nation, although at that point still a bloodless one. The bloodless battle is reinforced by the statement that:

> it is a battle that cannot be won by just bayonets and bullets. It is a battle of ideals and ideas. And the side that recruits more ability and talent will be the side that wins.

The words "battle won", "bayonets", "bullets", "side" and "wins" reinforce this metaphor of battle, which is further enhanced by the terms "combating" and "retreating", "struck", "gun" and "helicopters".

Summary of Analysis

Notably, this speech refers to the "PLEN's" interest not only in the nation of Singapore but also in the PAP. This shows the speaker's awareness that the "PLEN" viewed the PAP as a means to win the nation. Revealing this plan of the "PLEN" serves two functions:

1. It reminds the audience that the PAP is identified and recognised as the most credible leadership in Singapore even by her enemies who would deny her independence and democracy; and
2. It causes the audience to ponder over how Singapore's past had been inextricably intertwined with the PAP.

From this the audience could be expected to extrapolate that Singapore's future too should be inevitably intertwined with the party. The PAP and the nation, in the mind of the audience, could therefore be seen as one and the same.

This second function is very important as the nation needed a powerful unified leadership. To view the various political parties as just so many options in a department store would have proven disastrous to the survival of the nation. Thus, the gentle reminder that the PAP and the nation are one. The creation of this concept was undertaken sensitively by the speaker. He does not state this identification overtly, but the identification is created in the mind of the audience as the "PLEN" had plans for both the party and the nation, and would have used one to get to the other.

We must remember that this speech recalls a past event, and that the audience listening to the speech had witnessed the subsequent bloodshed and violence. Thus, as the audience listened and recalled, we can only speculate on their feelings – certainly feelings of relief that the "PLEN" had been handled so masterfully.

3. The Merger and Separation of Singapore and Malaya (1963–1965)

Historical Background

The Federation of Malaysia was formed on 16 September 1963, comprising the states of Malaya, Sarawak, Sabah and Singapore. At that time, the Prime Ministers of both Singapore and Malaya, Mr. Lee Kuan Yew and Tunku Abdul Rahman respectively, were confident that the merger and unity of Singapore and Malaya would work.

But on 9 August 1965, Singapore separated from Malaysia. Behind the Tunku's statement that this is the "most painful and heartbreaking news that I have had to break"[1], lay a variety of factors. What were these factors?

A study by Fletcher indicates three crucial reasons for the separation.[2] The first can be attributed to different contentions arising from the financial and economic aspects of the agreement. The differences in economic interests in the two states, specifically the interpretations of roles and goals of "the common market, the state-federal division of revenue, the Borneo loan [and] industrial and trade policies"[3], became points of conflict.

The second and third reasons leading to the separation of Malaysia and Singapore are closely intertwined. Fletcher cites the political ideas of Lee Kuan Yew as the second reason and the racial issue as the third reason. To Lee:

> Malaya was part of Malaysia, a federation to be run by Malaysians, no matter what colour or where they came from.

To the Tunku:

> Malaysia is for Malays and should not be governed by a mixture of races.[4]

Bloodworth summarises the crux of the political difference:

> A conservative, predominantly Malay government in Kuala Lumpur confronted a social democrat, predominantly Chinese government in Singapore, and while the more leisurely Malays accused the workaholic Chinese of plotting to cheat them of their heritage, the Chinese accused the Malays of plotting to cheat them of their rights as Malaysians. Both sides lost their tempers, and only one key to reconciliation remained – divorce.[5]

Before looking at the discourse aimed at sustaining the merger, it is helpful to look at the reasons for the merger, from Singapore's point of view. Such information will provide a useful backdrop in our understanding of the feelings and sentiments of the period.

According to Fletcher, the "PAP leaders saw merger as the only possible solution to Singapore's severe economic problems."[6] Singapore has no natural resources and relies solely on entrepot trade. Malaysia, on the other hand, had vast resources and its production of rubber and tin could facilitate faster industrial growth. Also, the size of Singapore's market is small and the merger of Singapore and Malaysia would provide a bigger market.

Another reason for Singapore's desire for the merger was the Communist Threat. The riots and strikes which the Communists initiated were a growing concern for the Singapore government. For one, Communist activities were on the rise. For another, Singapore would not be a conducive place for industrialization if potential investors perceived that the economy was not stable. If Singapore merged with Malaya, this Communist Threat would be at least somewhat diluted as the population in the Federation would be an even larger majority against the Communists.

Fletcher also suggested that a reason for the "PAP's desire for merger concerned the viability of Singapore as an independent state". Lee Kuan Yew thought that an independent Singapore would not be "politically, militarily or economically viable."[7] He feared that minute Singapore, devoid of economic strength, would be dwarfed by other economies in the region and find it impossible to survive.

The following speech will be analysed with this situation in mind, that Singapore had the fervent hope of sustaining merger in the midst of differences of attitudes towards how the new Malaysia was to be administered.

"Are There Enough Malaysians To Save Malaysia?"

Speech

This speech was delivered to the Medical Society by Lee Kuan Yew at the Pathology Department, General Hospital on 26 February 1965.

Source: *Are There Enough Malaysians To Save Malaysians?* (Singapore: Ministry of Culture, 1963–1965).

That I should have chosen as the title of this address 'Are there enough Malaysians to save Malaysia' is, in itself, an admission of the fact that we are, as surgeons will put it, very near the bone.

First, what is Malaysia; next, who wants Malaysia; next, who is *prepared* to fight and die for Malaysia?

I would like to start this discussion this evening *before* Malaysia was formed so that we can get quite clear in our minds *who* wanted Malaysia and *why*, because *why* they wanted Malaysia will decide whether they are prepared to fight for it, and if necessary, die for it.

There were three primary parties at the beginning: the Federation of Malaya Government – the Singapore Government, and the British Government. And as the discussion went on, there emerged gradually the will of the people of Sabah and Sarawak now more or less expressed in their State Governments.

What did the Federation of Malaya Government want Malaysia for? Only they can answer. But I would suggest that they were finally persuaded that they had

70 *Metaphor & Public Communication*

to integrate Singapore with Malaya because without it, the position would become so acute that their own security would be imperilled. Therefore, they had to have merger. And, for a diversity of reasons, they also wanted to have with Singapore, Sabah, Brunei and Sarawak to form Malaysia.

Why did the Singapore Government want Malaysia? If people in Malaysia understood *then* and understand *now* why we wanted Malaysia, and why we are prepared to fight for Malaysia – not for Singapore, not for Malaya, but for what we fought to achieve – then they will understand the alternatives that were open to us then. We wanted Malaysia because the alternative to Malaysia was a stage of constant instability in Southeast Asia in which the end result could have been something not very different from what has happened in Cuba, but with very different results. For if Singapore were left isolated in Malaysia, economically confined and conscribed, then there was only one way out for it to reach for freedom and fulfillment, and that was to play a Cuban role. The end result of such an effort would have been a very different situation in the whole of Southeast Asia.

However, we decided, and we carried with us the majority of the people of Singapore, to merge with Malaya, to try and form a multiracial society out of the many diverse peoples who were already here and those who came in the one hundred years of British rule into the territories now comprised in Malaysia.

To be honest, we would have been quite happy to have gone without Sabah, Sarawak or Brunei. For a diversity of reasons which really underlie the difference between the basic attitudes of the Federation of Malaya Government and the Singapore Government, merger was not possible unless these territories came in. So we went out of our way to persuade them to come in. Having been persuaded to come in, those who led their peoples into Malaysia are not likely to submit willingly to any form of hegemony which was not contemplated when Malaysia was founded.

Malaya did not want Singapore because . . . there was

a large non-Malay population, mainly Chinese. If this population were combined with Malaya, it would upset the demographic balance in Malaya. A very important factor for those who play politics along demographic lines but irrelevant to us, because our politics cuts across race, culture, religion, language.

You know the history of the last three and a half years since 1961. And you know therefore, why it was that Singapore went in on very special terms: to ease the sudden admixture of two relatively different textures of society. One was a conservative, static society wanting to keep what was in the past, wanting to reinforce the forces that kept the society where it was. The other was an innovating society, prepared to reach out for the stars, prepared to try and experiment, pick the best that would suit us. And if you had an admixture of these two suddenly, it might become quite a traumatic experience. For those reasons, we decided that it should be done in gradual phases. If you suddenly introduce the education policies, and the labour policies of Singapore and the social and ideological philosophies underlying them into the Malayan milieu, a traumatic shock may result.

Now, after 16 months of Malaysia, we have to face the realities of life brought about and accentuated by confrontation. What went wrong to happy and prosperous Malaysia? I say basically, confrontation, accentuating cultural, linguistic and other conflicts within the Malaysian society, resulted in the weakening of the will of those who set out to establish this Malaysian nation from going through with it.

You have watched the drift in events, the little manifestations of a lack of resolve. I had on an occasion to comment on Radio Malaysia calling Indonesian terrorists "Saudara". It started quite an argument on the etymology and the emotional connotation of words. What is more important is that from time to time we are reminded that we are fighting not so much what Indonesian confrontation represents, but the wicked Communists, the Partai Kominis Indonesia (Communist Party of Indonesia), the Chinese who are helping the Partai Kominis Indonesia who are using the Bung.

Well, that is in part true, but only in part. And what concerns us is that the hub of the problem is so sensitive that so many people in authority find it difficult to face up to the problem of whether Malaysia is worth preserving as it was ordained to be when we proclaimed it in September 1963: a Malaysian nation with provisos to look after the indigenous peoples to ensure that their cultural, their economic and their social advance in competition with more competitive people of immigrant stock are not jeopardized.

You have read in recent weeks a rise in the cacophony of politicians who talk about the same thing in different words and who use the same words to mean different things; of how, if one preaches non-communalism, in fact one is communal because it arouses communalism in some.

When the Constitution was promulgated, it provided for the system of one-man-one-vote, or to be exact, one-citizen-one-vote, because not all men in Malaysia have one vote. It is one-citizen-one-vote. It was a situation in which there was going to be a time lag of some 10, 15, 20 years before the full impact of one-man-one-vote was to be felt on the political life of the country. We knew it; the Federation of Malaya Government knew it; the people of Sarawak by and large knew it; and so did Sabah. So did Brunei, and they decided to opt out.

What did that Constitution imply? First, that there were to be different speeds at which Malaya, Singapore, Sabah, Sarawak were to advance because they were in different stages of development. The weighting was in Malaya, the founder member, and the weighting in Malaya was with the rural areas by virtue of citizenship laws which were promulgated in 1957 when the country became independent. Singapore took a weighting in the centre which was below what it was entitled to in return for more freedom of action to continue to move faster in its own style and in its fashion than Malaya, and to allow time to decide when complete integration would be advisable and possible. Similarly, Sarawak and Sabah being less advanced administratively and politically than Malaya, the founder member, were given certain

The Merger and Separation of Singapore and Malaya 73

added weightings in the centre: 40 seats for 1.2 million people which, in Johore, would have entitle them to 20 or less seats; they were given 40 seats, and a certain degree, not so much as Singapore, of local autonomy, and a promise of economic assistance to accelerate development.

Anybody reading the Constitution must accept that over the years, 10, 15, 20 years, unless he is prepared to break the Constitution, a point will be reached when everybody born in this country will be a citizen and will have the vote; when the economic integration of the country will become closer until it is complete; and when there will be an ironing out of the disparities between States and between communities within our society. That was something we accepted. In fact, we undertook, to help the centre to help the development of Sabah and Sarawak by promising loans, (some ⅓ interest-free, ⅔ bearing 5½ percent or whatever the current market rate would be), of a 150 million dollars over a period of five years.

Then came confrontation. Without confrontation, the history of Malaysia would have been different. But then, the history of the whole of Southeast Asia would have been different because confrontation put on Malaysia pressures which generated divisive forces within the community. It was as if Malaysia were Hainan Island and suddenly the local leader found himself in competition with a great orator in the Chinese People's Republic making a direct bid for 4½ million people on Hainan Island. And the leaders of the 4½ million people on Hainan Island did not feel sufficiently confident to tell their following that whatever ethnic and other linguistic or cultural history they shared with the mainland, some five and more million peoples had come during the last 100 odd years, and created quite a heterogeneous society which must be slowly interwoven.

There were two choices open to any leadership in that situation to meet Indonesian confrontation. One was to say: what about the Majapahit, the Sri Vijaya Empires, what about all this? For the last 300 odd years, you were under Dutch rule, we were under British rule: Our destinies had parted. Today, vaguely we are akin in some respects, speaking a language broadly similar, but not the same; and living a much better life because in our midst, over a 100 odd years of British rule, some five to six million people came to help our country progress. Our destinies lie with them. Let us compete and see who provides his country and his people with a better life. On that competition, if those were the terms of reference of the competition, Malaysia must win, because we can always keep ahead, always give our people a better life.

But if you try and compete with President Sukarno on who can give his people a greater future as a *Malay* people, one promising the renaissance of Sri Vijaya, Majapahit Empires, greatness stretching across the whole of South Asia between the Indian Ocean and the Pacific, between the northern and southern hemispheres, and the other just an adjunct of this mosaic in Southeast Asia, then you must lose. It is a competition which, we should not attempt because it is not a competition that can be won.

I do not know what the destiny of the 105 million peoples of Indonesia may be. It could become a very great nation. It could so very easily splinter up into so many island empires once the present leader has passed away, and lost the capacity to mesmerize these people into feeling one. We do not know; and it is not within our dispensation to decide these things. We wish the Indonesian people well.

But I do know that it is utter folly to try and compete with them as to which one will provide the greater Malay civilization. There are 4½ million Malays here, and 90 million Malays on the other side; so you must lose. They have got 105 million people, but about 15 million of them are Dayaks and Amboyanese and other groups who are not Malays, and probably more millions who are not Muslims. It is an unequal contest.

Because of these sudden pressures, it is possible that a qualitative change took place over the last one and a half years, probably beginning slightly before Malaysia when the pressure was mounted, in the nature of leadership within the country. The tolerant, easygoing society suddenly came under acute pressures. And the conflicts became acute, most significantly after the general elections in Malaya were over, April last year. Then they thought there were five years ahead, and things could be put in order and sorted out, and time can elapse for things to be forgotten before the next casting of the vote. What was more important, in the process of the elections, the second-tier leaders realized their importance – that they, not the Ministers, they, the people who addressed the mass rallies, who spoke the patois of the kampung folk, it was they who rallied the masses. And they had very different ideas about what the nature or the texture of Malaysia should be.

The Ministers who had to negotiate Malaysia knew full well, I must assume this because they were intelligent, rational men, they knew full well what it was they were taking on. When they did not want Singapore by itself, they did not want a Malaysia in which Chinese chauvinism could pay, or where there could be Chinese dominance. Without the Borneo territories, it is possible, working one-citizen-one-vote, to have an appeal to one single community; just an appeal directly to Chinese chauvinism could carry the day.

I sympathize with that point of view; and we never intended to operate on the basis of Chinese chauvinism and we did not desire a Chinese-dominated Malaysia. If we did, we would never have gone into merger and would have tried to achieve our objectives the other way which some people wanted to do: a separate Singapore which subsequently *must* come into conflict with Malaya, in which supremacy depends upon who has greater strength.

We thought it was by far more sensible and certainly had a better chance of success if we did it this way: a gradual process of integration. We assumed that they wanted 1.2 million people largely of native stock, Dayaks, Dusuns, Kelabits, Muruts, Kenyans, Kadazans, Ibans because they wanted to negate any bias towards a Chinese chauvinist Malaysia, and we say, all to the good. It never occurred to us that anybody working out this arithmetic could imagine that in this particular framework, he could operate in the same way as he did in Malaya because the basis had altered.

But after the elections, we discovered over the months to our amazement, incredulity and subsequent horror, that in fact they believed they could force Malaysia into the Malaysian pattern. This, in my submission, is an impossibility. If I were asked to do it, I would refuse because I know it is not possible.

I will tell you the dilemma which these second-tier leaders face. I call them the ultras. They call themselves the ultra-nationalists. These people are attempting to shroud this country with a pattern which vaguely they were attempting in Malaya and which I doubt whether they would succeed in establishing even in Malaya itself. For you to understand this, I would like first to try and put you in the picture as to what was happening all these years in Malaya.

Every time I quote percentages, they say, "Ah, he is being communal." But I quote these percentages to remind those who are working on the basis of the percentages of old Malaya that it is a folly to persist on these assumptions because those assumptions no longer apply; and every time they are reminded of that, they go into a fit.

In old Malaya, there were 50 percent Malays. But because of the immigrant population being, by and large, recent, they constituted 65 percent of the vote, and the other 50 percent of the population made up 35 percent of the vote.

In that situation, anybody who obtained the support of the majority of the 65 percent automatically could, and did, assume majority of the whole. And it is not difficult to get the majority of the 65 percent to cluster together because they saw, how in the years of the Emergency . . . they felt anxious about the future when an insurrection took place led largely by immigrant Chinese. They feared and were encouraged to fear, that if it succeeded, it would mean their being overwhelmed and subdued and subjugated.

Whether it is true or not, that's another matter which we'll discuss on another occasion. But now they are saying that even if *any* of these people of immigrant stock share in supremacy in the ballot, then the 65 percent will be subdued and we are spending our time trying to prove that that is not so. And the more we attempt to prove that is not so, and the more we succeed, the angrier they become.

Those in power had only the Pan-Malayan Islamic Party to contend with. The Pan-Malayan Islamic Party tried to play a more Malay line, and took away perhaps 15, 20 percent out of the 65 percent leaving behind 45, maybe 50 percent. One can have separate guesses if one does the statistical analysis of the election results. On the other side, the 35 percent, there were a multitude of parties to chop them all up, so they were quite sure of winning. Socialist Front, and then you divide the Socialist Front into Labour Party and Party Rakyat; then Malayan Indian Congress; and as if that is not enough, you had the Peoples Progressive Party, and you have the Malayan Party and the United Democratic Party; and of course, you have always got a convenient organization called the Malayan Chinese Association which represents the Chinese; and so it generally helps to splinter up the 35 percent. So if you can go on playing this game at *ad infinitum*: you might be in power forever after. So the theory goes.

In fact, the theory suffers from one very serious defect in that it does not take into account that the society, even Malaya by itself, has a logic and a momentum of its own: there's a social upheaval going on even within that society. But the impact of Singapore, not just in percentage terms but in terms of ideas and example, was a traumatic experience.

We believed, and we still believe, that the best future for this country lies in gradual integration of our communities into a *Malaysian* society. The alternative is ultimate disintegration into its component parts, and worse, perhaps not even into its component parts. Because, if you have a division on the basis of race, language, religion, the country will be unzipped right down the middle. And it is very difficult to divide town from country.

Whilst all this argument was going on and the Communists through Barisan Sosialis, Socialist Front and Sarawak United People's Party in Sarawak all said that it was a sell-out – in fact, a great deal of calculation, recalculations were done as to what was going to be the final sephological effect, the effect on voting, of such a system on the future of Malaysia. We were quite confident that given 10, 15, 20 years, a Malaysian nation *must* emerge provided one-citizen-one-vote obtained.

If, of course, you should decide to scrap the one-citizen-one-vote, then, there are many other possible results. It depends upon what happens with our neighbours: how much our neighbours interfere in our affairs to the north, to the south. It might end up in all kinds of curious permutations and combinations, partition and so on. We believe the gradual process of integration is the best for us.

Then Malaysia came. We were quite sure that that must be so. Lo and behold, for the first time in the history of elections, three Malay constituencies in Singapore voted for a *non*-Malay-led party, non-Malay in the sense that the top leaders were not Malays. This was something which could not be tolerated if their perpetual dominance was to be assured. If the same processes of the social and the economic programme winning over Malays, Chinese, Indians, Ceylonese, Pakistanis, Eurasians, and others into *one* multi-racial movement were allowed into Malaysia, then, the old theory of working on the 65 percent – whoever holds the majority of the 65 percent holding the country – breaks down. If part of the 65 percent joins the others in a multiracial party, then what happens?

The first attempt was made purely as a negative move to ensure that this process will never set in for a long, long time, if possible never, in Malaya. People who were doing better than anybody else, than any other kampung folk in Malaya, were told that they were being oppressed, chased out of the towns, kampungs, persecuted and oppressed. And, out of 250,000 people, you can always find 200 chaps who are prepared to have a go. It is not difficult: even in a cowed situation like Kuala Lumpur, Socialist Front got 2,000 people to march down Batu Road.

This has gone for one year, nearly ten months. It was our belief that if they were given time, perhaps they would expend their efforts, accept the inevitable in that this thing has already been *agreed*: that it shall be so, that over a process of 15, 20 years, there must be a Malaysian nation. We had reasons to believe on past performance that the top leadership would check the vagaries and excesses of the ground leadership.

But the day I read that *Utusan Melayu* was elevated as the "Voice of the Malays", that day I was sadly disillusioned. I then realized that, under conditions of confrontation, it is not possible to expect this leadership to exercise the same modulating and moderating influence that it had over the years since 1955.

When you have a very great orator making a very big appeal – then the temptation to try to be *as* good as the other chap is very great. And if you can't make a speech that can enthrall them, then at least you should try and pretend that you are going to do as much for them as Malays as the other fellow is *not*, because he is selling out Malayism, culture, religion and so on to the Partai Kominis Indonesia Communists, Chinese Communists, Russian Communists.

We go back again to the terms of reference under which the competition could take place. The terms of reference could be: let us see who can give their people a better life, a better future for themselves and their offspring. *Or*, it could be which is the greater Malay nation. And I have explained why, it is not possible, in these circumstances, to outbid them. Therefore, I would prefer to compete on who could give a country a better life, and their people a better future. I am quite sure whatever renaissance they have in store in Indonesia, whether it is *one* renaissance or separate renaissances, they have a period of very great trial and tribulation and privation ahead, whoever takes over, whether it is the Communists, the army or whatever other forces that are left behind in Indonesia when the President is no longer there.

But when you try and compete, and when you have got a few little chaps who think they can make great speeches like Sukarno – and they have been round to the kampungs rallying these people on lines which promise them a future as a *separate* people from the others in the community – then you are reluctant, or you feel inhibited, in asserting what you know to be right, because there are political perils involved. As I said, if I were in Hainan Island competing with Mao Tse Tung, I would feel a little bit inhibited. I concede that.

But, it is no use our pretending that these things do not exist, and it is no use pretending, like the Communists, that this is a neo-colonialist plot and if only we destroy Malaysia, all would be well. I am quite sure that all would *not* be well, and we would all be in dire peril. And that we must find a way out through sheer perseverance, patience and determination to see that there are enough Malaysians to save Malaysia.

The magic formula no longer works. Whoever has the majority of the 65 percent governs, but whoever contains the majority of the 65 has the majority only of 104 seats in Parliament. There are the other 40 Borneo seats plus 15 Singapore seats, that's 55. So whoever loses 25 to the other side, there's 25 plus 55 makes 80, which is one over half of 159.

To get the majority of the 65 percent in old Malaya in which the total was 104 seats and, whoever gets the majority of the 65 percent votes wins, you can afford to take a pretty hard line against the 35 percent. There are such a multitude of champions who say that they can save the 35 percent that they are confused and they don't know which one really would give them the pills that will send them to euphoria, so you chop them all up. You hold your majority of 65, you are in; and 35 in any case understand that within the 104, they are out.

The Merger and Separation of Singapore and Malaya 81

You then export that technique to a situation where in the Singapore State Assembly of 51 seats, you work on 12 percent! I would have thought anybody who sat down with pencil and paper would have told them that the end result must be quite different. But they actually set out to work on 12 percent to win what cannot be more than three seats; to be quite certain, that they lost 48. It would have been worth it if they *could* have provoked a multiracial party into taking an anti-Malay or an anti-Malay special rights stand because then they would have sealed us off forever from that 65 percent in Malaya.

But every time they provoked us, we say, well, what more can we do? We are determined that we shall do what is right by our fellow countrymen, regardless of race, language or religion, who are less privileged than the others. What is more, we believe not in giving largesse, gold coins, but in increasing a man's worth and his capacity to earn, and making him a more self-respecting human being. And we are prepared to pay that price over a very long period.

If we for one moment slipped up, lost our temper and reacted as some people had been made to react in Malaya, to say, "Down with all these feudalists, or down with Malay special rights," they would have sat back with great relief because we were going to be for a long time sealed off.

But we said, "Yes, what more? RIDA (Rural and Industrial Development Authority) coming to Singapore? Please do. Every assistance to you. Housing cooperatives to help the poor rehouse themselves? By all means: selling at cost. Housing and Development Board Estate ready, waiting for sale. What more?" And so we will go on because it is worth our while going on to build a Malaysian nation which we believe is the only way out.

Meanwhile, not having sat down with pencil and paper to make quite sure of the sephological weightings in this, they merrily pursued this line which set off chain emotions in people which ended up with their own people wanting to eat up their own creatures. Chief

Minister of Penang, Mr. Wong Pow Nee, good Christian, holy man, humble man, was attacked. "Bad man," say they; did not attend some function about language week. Dr. Lim Swee Aun, bad man, anti-Malaysian because he said Malays should work hard in business and succeed, and should not do so at the expense of the others.

You see, you have generated these emotions. That's a logic and momentum in communal politics. Your ground, not understanding what you were doing these things for, believe really that Chinese generally must be wicked people. If you start telling them yes, beware of these Chinamen, then they say, yes, that's right, look at that Malayan Chinese Association Minister, he is a Chinaman. And he was denounced because he could not keep the price of sugar and other things from going up because the policy of the government was implemented by his own colleague, another Chinaman, was designed to increase the price of commodities. How can you blame the poor man? My heart bled for him so I came out and said, "Why should you do these things to him?" And now the Finance Minister having told us in Parliament that all this was being taxed, all this turnover, payroll tax was to squeeze money out of the rich to help the country advance – goes to a meeting of his own rich clientele in the Malayan Chinese Association and says, "Those of you who can't pass the tax on to the others, please let me know, we'll exempt you. But if you can pass it on, there is no question of hardship, because the poor chaps in the kampungs, make them pay."

This is the dilemma they are faced with. And this is the real problem we face in Malaysia. How long can we afford to allow what is basically an economic and social problem to be cloaked over by all this communal claptrap?

They have been in authority since 1955. You know what the Professor of Economics in the University of Malaya thinks about rural development, so I am not here to go over his ground. But I am quite sure, if you look up the social register "Who is Who?", the big commercial Red

Book, you will now definitely find more members of the aristocracy and the elite amongst the company directors. I concede that. They are sharing spoils with their counterparts. And why not? If you can keep the ground befuddled, you carry this on indefinitely; and every time they get restive after a while when they discover that they are no better off, you say, "Ah yes, these wicked chaps, the Chinese, you know, they exploit us. Give us more than 25 percent shares, make it 50 percent now." So the 50 percent is shared amongst the same elite. So the poor chaps on the ground, after four, five years realize that something is gone wrong, because it is the same as before, so they say, make it 75 percent then. More directors: that's the way to solve it! Have classes to teach Malays how to be contractors: then we solve it, you see? All the chaps who would otherwise go into revolution, go madly spinning around tenders to make money; and the problem is solved.

It has not even been solved thus here, but I tell you how it's being solved: by keeping the society static, by reinforcing those instincts, those learnt reflexes in your community which keep it from changing too quickly. So, from nine Sultans, we have nine Sultans and one Agong. This serves a definite political function with the kampung people, and we must recognize this as such. You pin down the traditional loyalties of the people. Then, to reinforce it, you have a systematic scheme, paid for by the lotteries fund, to build little mosques all over the country, I am told that that's contrary to beliefs of some of the people who attend these mosques, but nevertheless, a definite purpose has been served.

What is curious is that the Middle Eastern countries that are advancing today, the United Arab Republic for instance, are the countries that broke up the Muslim brotherhood, the conservative forces that held a society down. You *must* be an innovating society. You must be prepared to reach out for the stars; hence, the Aswan Dam. You are proud of your Pyramids but you get on and learn how to move granite to collect water, to irrigate your fields, to produce power, to produce your fertilizers and so on.

Having operated on this very confined basis, for eight long years within the framework of Malaya, they attempted it in Malaysia without calculating the price. But *this* time, not only did they lose out in this Singapore situation, where 88 percent on the other side control 48 out of 51 seats, but they never intended to win the majority of the 51 except for one flickering moment when they made an attempt, because to win the majority of the 51, they had to alter their outlook basically and radically and become Malaysian.

When they sent down Malayan Chinese Association ministers and Malayan Indian Congress ministers to go into the field in Singapore, we were happy because we felt if only they would try... in the process of trying, they must become Malaysians.

Over the last few weeks, we knew that the attempt has been abandoned. They were not prepared to pay the price to make a Malaysian appeal and compete. They wanted to work on their old formula. And, what is worse, they did not calculate the impact of operating their old formula on their *own* 35 percent in the new circumstances. Because you don't just alienate Singapore: when you come down and say "urban pride" and "lucky thing the rural areas do not know of your arrogance," you are taking on a large section of the population. You are not just saying, "Singapore you so and so," but you are saying, "Urban areas, you so and so," with repercussions on Sabah and Sarawak which must mean, in the end, a very major rearrangement of the forces *within* Malaysia which can end with very dramatic results if the one-man, one-citizen-one-vote continues.

Naturally, this brings to our mind the question of whether in that event, the system of one-citizen-one-vote will continue.

I feel reasonably confident that within this particular situation, when the whole world is focussed on Malaysia, it is *not* possible for them to scrap, without disastrous consequences, the system of one-citizen-one-vote. You see, let's take it both ways. Assume first that you can scrap this system and have the capacity to govern it as it has been governed in Pakistan or in Burma or in Thailand. Let's assume first there is the capacity – of course, my next premise is there is no such capacity – but let us assume that there is: The end result of that capacity must mean a gradual erosion of all semblance of popular support, and the emergence of strident, militant opposition that will end up with real internecine strife, ending up in the conquest of one side over the other. And I do not have to tell you what history teaches us in those respects.

But worse, there is not even the capacity to sustain it if you scrap the system. You are dependent for survival on three popular democracies; and I mean 'popular' in the real sense of the term: popularly-elected governments, British, Australian and New Zealander. Without them, Malaysia cannot survive. It is not worth our while expending all this effort to counter Indonesia's constant pressures because it will break us in the end: we have not got the capacity. You must have friends to support you. And these friends support you because it is in their interest to do so, not out of charity. Never make the error of believing that the world owes you a living because it does not. It does not owe us a living. They support us in so far as their interests militate that they should; that an independent, separate Malaysia, separate from Indonesia, is something desirable in itself. The Australians are being drawn into it more and more – one battalion going out to Sabah; engineers had gone out beforehand and over the next five, ten years, more and more Australian commitment is inevitable. The British know it as the Australians know it because they have more interests involved. So with the New Zealanders. They have their interests involved because it is worse for them ultimately if under these circumstances, Malaysia were allowed to be overwhelmed by Indonesia. Under these circumstances, they will support Malaysia *provided* you have got here a democratic *viable* system being attacked and they can stand up to the world and say: "I am doing my duty as a good neighbour and fellow member of the Commonwealth to protect the independence of my younger brother, mind you, for many various important interest of my own, but nevertheless, here is somebody worth defending."

But if it were to become somebody which became an embarrassment to defend, what happens? I am quite sure they are intelligent enough to know that it is a very foolish thing to get involved in a second Vietnam where the political basis has disappeared. You know, it is very important, this Lieutenant-General Minh or whatever his name is ... he is a former member of the Viet-Minh ... he said *why* did Diem collapse, why did the generals after him collapse? The corruption and the decadence of the society could not rally the people. And any western or Australian power will think twice before they find themselves married and wedded to a completely outmoded regime.

They would not want to be committed to that situation where the political jell and the political basis of multi-racial Malaysia is split asunder as a result of extreme communal politicking. And, even assuming that the governments were foolish enough to be involved, to continue and expend their national effort to defend such a Malaysia, I do not believe that their people will let them. And they have periodic elections: every five years at the latest in Britain; every three years at the latest in Australia and New Zealand. This so ordained by law. And you might have it at more frequent intervals too.

My conclusion is that it pays us to be patient; to be tolerant and to be flexible; but never to waver or to yield on fundamentals. And Malaysia as a Malaysian nation is a fundamental. And if there are enough of us who are prepared to give expression to our desire to see that such a nation emerges and flourishes, it cannot but have a salutary effect not only within the country, but also amongst our neighbours who do their calculations on the basis of what they think is likely to happen within the country, and equally important amongst our friends, who for their own reasons, are expending a great deal of their effort to sustain us.

And let us not miscalculate what it means to them. The

British have been doing this for hundreds of years, 400 years of empire, but for the Australians, this is the first agonizing step they have taken in peacetime; conscription in peacetime. An affluent society now forced to face up to the facts of life in Southeast Asia and intelligent enough to understand that it *is* in South Asia, the southern-most part of South Asia, and that it is better to take an interest now than to find themselves presented with a *fait accompli* later.

But what we must never forget is this: that the Australians, as the Prime Minister of Australia said, have got to live with one hundred million Indonesians for "hundreds of year" as he said. And people don't go out of their way to take a stand which will antagonize a neighbour of a hundred million odd people, ten times their own number, just to humour a friendly regime, humour a traditional leader or a prince. Taking a stand may mean your own future with your neighbour. Like us they do their calculations, everyday, if not twice a day; and when it is not worth their while, they must, as the Americans under similar circumstances must, cut their losses.

The tragedy of our situation is that on our own, we have not the capacity to make Malaysia succeed. We need the cooperation of those who lead the 65 percent to make it succeed. But we are quite certain that if anybody decides that they should scrub us out, we have the capacity... or if we have not got the capacity, the people have the capacity, to scrub out the whole of Malaysia. Nobody is the winner. I am not even sure whether the Indonesians would be the winner because one doesn't know what the ultimate result will be in a free-for-all because, in that situation, it must become a free-for-all.

It is your ground situation, the loyalties of your people, their beliefs in that it is worthwhile helping authority to keep this down. Once they feel a sense of insecurity as a result of malevolent authority and their sympathies are with the other side, then I say disintegration begins.

Gentlemen, I am not morbid by nature, and I do not like to generate euphoria. But I think it is necessary from time to time, that we should sometimes speak unhappily of some of the very unfortunate things which have happened in the hope that in so doing, we bring realization of the basic facts of life and the dilemma we are all confronted with in time to prevent people from doing things detrimental to their own interests.

In the long run, if we are able to find enough Malaysians to save Malaysia, then we must have Malaysian parties, or Malaysian movements; Malaysian thought, a Malaysian body of opinion which cut across race, language and religion. And you represent a small but not insignificant force.

In the English-educated stream, whatever its other weaknesses, there was a confluence of experiences, thoughts, and, I hope, ideals and similar values. At the same time, there are the other different streams of life, the Chinese-educated, and the Malay-educated. One of the problems before Malaysia, in Singapore was the unthinking dominance and assertion of a group of the Chinese-educated that did not see beyond Singapore and only saw Singapore, unable to realize the milieu in which we are imprisoned in Southeast Asia. Now, we find, the converse position. There are a few people who believe that the hegemony of one group can be established because they are in authority; and they are quite oblivious or refuse to accept the fact that with Singapore, Sabah and Sarawak, Malaya became qualitatively, a very different country altogether. That their technique of the communally-segregated party which ensured their perpetual dominance no longer operates.

You saw the newspapers this morning: A Federal Minister went to Sabah and told the Chinese, "Don't waste your strength; unite, support so and so party." And you read the newspapers yesterday about the Prime Minister of Malaysia giving an interview. He says, "What is wrong? Malays will cooperate with the Chinese and Indians, UMNO, MCA and MIC."

Now, I don't want to be a heretic. I would like to accommodate, and try and more slowly evolve things but I think I'd like to point this out. And I have already had it said to me before and I put it in the newspapers once last year that I was told it is all right if I discussed all these things with University students because they are thinking chaps. They won't run amok, but it is very bad if I tell this to the multitude at large. Who decides who represents the Chinese? If we really take the Federal Minister literally, the man who went to Sabah, and he is quite a very nice gentleman, Dr. Lim Swee Aun, we take him at his words, "Chinese unite . . ." Really? You really want that? Don't you think the whole thing will be in peril? It is all right if the Malayan Chinese Association says, "Chinese unite". If the People's Action Party says, "Malaysians unite", it is already wrong, let alone "Chinese unite".

You can only operate this . . . this magic formula within the Malayan framework. You pour in Singapore, Sabah and Sarawak – 20 different nationalities in Sabah and Sarawak alone – and the magic formula no longer works. And let me advise the Indians and the Chinese never do a silly thing like Indians unite with Indians and Chinese unite with Chinese. Not only is it disastrous for the country but you can't win. It is a waste of time trying to do that. Malaysians unite, you *will* win. And if you go home with a piece of paper and you look up your geography book, and look up the annual statistics and annual reports of the three territories, do sephological exercise, you will know why when I say "Malaysians unite", Malaysians *can* win. But if you get caught just in the Chinese world, and say "Chinese unite", then you deserve, by your stupidity to be so quarantined and isolated and destroyed.

Are we able, over the next few months, to find some adjustment which will take the acuteness and anxiety out of the situation? The anxiety of those who have been working this formula and now discover belatedly that, in fact, the formula no longer works in Malaysia.

When you start going for the urban people and talk of urban pride, and this, that and the other, you jell all the other urban chaps outside Singapore together. There is a logic of action and interaction in communalism, and you start doing these silly things, you set a chain reaction. And they bring down upon themselves the very thing they wanted to avoid: the unity of those who want a multiracial society. So the 35 percent are no longer cowed and intimidated. They no longer believe that they must cooperate with whoever holds the majority of the 65 percent because they now know that they are not just caught in 35 percent, that a whole vista opens up before them.

Now this, I concede is a very unpleasant discovery for those who have worked on the basis that the old magic can carry on. And therefore, I suggest, all should take time and reflect on these things and we should find some *modus vivendi* to take the heat out of the situation. Some adjustments must be made in order that all shall have time to decide whether it is worthwhile having Malaysia as it is, because there is no other way. There is no other Malaysia possible. All other Malaysias you have got to do by force, and there isn't sufficient force. And anyway, it is not possible to do it for multifarious other reasons.

If we decide that it is worth it, and there are enough people cutting across all racial, all religious, all linguistic lines, who believe that this multi-racial nation is worth having because it gives the best society, the best standards of life in Asia, tolerance, accommodation in a relatively prosperous society, then the adjustments will automatically be made and the battle will be fought against poverty, inequality between 'haves' and 'have-nots'.

The tragedy in which I, as a socialist, find myself is this: that as at this given moment, the 'haves' can still confuse the 'haves-nots' by talking about Malay rights, National Language and so on. The National Language is not going to solve rural poverty. The fact that you and I tomorrow meet and speak to each other in the National Language, which I hope one day will take place, is not going to solve inadequate research on agriculture and crop cultivation, marketing facilities, and institutions, which can increase the capacity to earn of an agricultural and a fishing people.

They can't solve it and it cannot be solved by fiscal and financial policies of those who have got vast rubber interests, vast wealth, whose preoccupation is the preservation of the structure of a society in which they make that wealth bigger. It cannot be done. Hence, the anguish of the argument in the last Budget: that this communally-segregated cooperation between three parties produced a Budget in which the second partner contrived very successfully to pass the burdens on to both the 'have-nots' of his first partner and of himself, race wise.

Does it really matter when you buy a coca-cola, whether you are a Chinese or a Malay or an Indian? You pay five cents for the crown cork. That money could have been found in many other ways in which the Chinese company director and the Malay in receipt of large allowances will pay for the economic upliftment of both the new villages and the old kampungs. That is the only solution.

Whatever the interim processes are, that is the only final solution. And I preach democratic socialism and an evolving society as a less painful way to reach that result. I am convinced that a static society cannot compete with the innovating society; and that our problem now, being people who believe in innovation, is to be patient, to try and let it progress by evolution and not by revolution.

Metaphoric Analysis

This speech was delivered by Lee Kuan Yew in Kuala Lumpur, Malaysia, on 26 February 1965. With hindsight, we know that it was given about five and a half months before the separation of Singapore from Malaya, when Singapore was still part of Malaya. In the transition from Malaya to Malaysia, there had been some difficulties concerning basic attitudes and policies towards Malaysia. In an effort to sustain merger and grow a Malaysia where there would be ample opportunities for all, Lee asks the question:

Are There Enough Malaysians to Save Malaysia?

The metaphoric analysis of this speech will focus on the locations to which Lee refers. The allusion to these locations has metaphoric pragmatics and carries considerable metaphoric import. Lee's use of metaphors is not overtly noticeable. But the references to the various locations do form a cluster of metaphors that is subservient to an overarching metaphoric concept – ie. a country is not just a geographical entity, but has socio-cultural pragmatics. To use Lakoff and Johnson's terms, this metaphor could be expressed as:

A nation is not just a geographical locality.

Lee begins the speech by pointing out that one reason Malaya was interested in the formation of Malaysia was the security issue. If Malayans were not for merger, "their own security would be imperilled." On the other hand, Singapore was desirous of a Malaysia so that it would not become "a state of constant instability in Southeast Asia in which the end result could have been something not very different from what [had] happened in Cuba".

Cuba is alluded to because of its history of political and social upheaval. The Castro regime transformed the island into a Communist state. To which aspect of Cuba is Lee alluding? Lee was probably alluding to the takeover of the island from the leadership of Fulgencio Batista. Fidel Castro led the takeover bid and even though the attempt to overthrow Batista failed, he became prominent. After his exile in Mexico, he returned to Cuba to launch another attack on Batista. Eventually, Batista's army collapsed before a powerful guerrilla army led by Castro. Batista fled and Castro came to power. Even though Castro's leadership was at first moderately democratic, it became increasingly extremist and revolutionary. He did not keep his promises of elections and those who opposed him were either killed or exiled. In 1961, the United States led the "Bay of Pigs" invasion but failed. Cuba became an ally of the Soviet Union. This alliance resulted in the dramatic Cuban Missile Crisis in 1962 – the Soviet Union had installed nuclear missiles on Cuba. The Soviet Union did this to protect Castro, to discredit the United States and to exert a more advantageous political position in that area.

Lee recognised that Singapore had the potential to become another Cuba in Southeast Asia. The Communists in Cuba had overthrown the prevailing government, exercised an authoritarian form of leadership and allowed the Soviet Union to use the country as a base for medium-range nuclear missiles. Lee asserts that Singapore desired merger so that it could be more stable than Cuba. At the same time, Malaysia too wanted a stable Singapore to ensure that the region would be more secure, in the light of the Communist Threat.

Thus, Lee uses Cuba as a metaphorical

referent to portray the potential turmoil that Singapore might face, as history had revealed. The threat of Communist invasion was real. If it had happened in Cuba, it could happen in Singapore. Cuba was many times the size of Singapore – 1200 km long and 97 km wide. If the Communist guerillas were capable of overthrowing the government of an island many times the size of Singapore, surely, Singapore too could be in a similarly perilous situation? Besides, the strategic location of Singapore could be used by any superpower to assert its might by way of a tool of domination as treacherous as missile installations.

Lee also refers to Hainan Island. The metaphoric reference to Hainan Island works in the same way as Cuba. Hainan Island demands that the audience recall history, and is used especially to illustrate the difficulties the leaders of Hainan Island faced when "a great orator in the Chinese People's Republic [made] a direct bid for four and a half million people on Hainan island." The point is that Hainan Island, which is inhabited by predominantly Hakka people and those of the aboriginal Li and Miao tribes, felt a cultural pull towards the mainland but at the same time, during the past one hundred years, grew up in a "heterogenous society which must be slowly interwoven". This dilemma is akin to whether we want a new Malaysia or whether we want everyone to return to his racial roots and thereby jeopardize a harmonious, multiracial society.

Recalling Cuba and Hainan Island in the speech underlined the primary historical events as well as the tumultuous quest for ideology. Lee makes good use of these geographical metaphors in a way that is more effective than painting a specific scenario about what might happen to Singapore and Malaysia if merger had not been accomplished and sustained. If a picture can speak a thousand words, the recalling of a geographical metaphor properly contextualised provides parallel, political pictures that capture the mind's eye in a dramatic way.

The third location is Malaysia. Lee makes it clear that Malaysia does not refer to just a geographical location, but also a concept or ideal. This is apparent in his question: "What is Malaysia...?" Other expressions that point to the fact that "Malaysia" can be seen to have metaphorical pragmatics include "an admixture" of a "conservative, static society" and "innovating society". Malaysia is thus thought of as a society that has been synthesised from two very different preexisting societies. The concept of this society was "ordained", reinforcing the idea of the creation of a new society for a special purpose. This metaphor works to emphasize that Malaysia was not like some country already in existence, with a long past that would determine its present and future situations. Another aspect of this conceptual society is "one-citizen-one-vote". In contrasting this to the phrase "one-man-one-vote", the speaker reinforces the idea of civic belonging and partisanship. Malaysia is a special concept that honours the vote of those who are committed to it.

Malaysia is spoken of as also having "nature" or "texture". Here the language that hints at Malaysia as a concept is replaced by the reference to Malaysia as a manifestation of an ideal. Lee mentions that different people had varying opinions about what the nature and texture of Malaysia should be, so that here Malaysia has a palpable reality. Thus, Malaysia is not an "airy-fairy" ideal, but one that can be created, as evidenced by the fact that people had differing ideas about Malaysia in its palpable form.

The metaphorical concept that a country is more than a geographical location receives further support from the statement that Lee prefers to compete with Indonesia on the basis of "who could give a country a better life, and their people a better future". This statement contributes the terms "life" and "future" to the key metaphorical concept of what constitutes a country. These two terms, with their own gestalts, remind the audience that a country is a living, growing thing that leads to a future. The gestalt for "life" would include "growth", "development", "fragility" and "nurturing". All of these terms envelop the concept of the country with associations of promise for the future. The term "future" suggests a gestalt that includes "promise" and "hope". The audience thus thinks of Malaysia as having the possibility of a desirable future.

In presenting the concept of Malaysia, Lee is careful to refer to the politics that is a necessary part of the ideal for a nation. Thus, he refers to the "political jell" and the "political basis" of Malaysia. The "jell" or factor that holds the nation together, as well as the "basis" or foundation of the nation, is a non-communal multiracialism. If communalism or sectarianism were allowed to flourish, this "jell" can easily be permanently destroyed, as implied by "split asunder".

Thus, when Lee later makes the assertion that: "Malaysia as a Malaysian nation is a fundamental", the term "Malaysia" refers to the name of a country, but "Malaysian" refers to the concept of the innovative, multiracial, one-citizen-one-vote situation, which has hope of a good future and life. Suddenly, the title of the speech referring to Malaysians saving Malaysia takes on a deeper meaning. Malaysians would be those who embody the ideals of this concept of Malaysia:

> We must have Malaysian parties, or Malaysian movements; Malaysian thought, a Malaysian body of opinion which cuts across race, language, and religion.

Along these lines, Malaysians would espouse the politics, ideas and thoughts that further the ideals of Malaysia as a multiracial future of promise and hope.

The speaker further asserts:

> There is no other Malaysia possible. All other Malaysias you have got to do by force.

This drives home the point further that a nation is more than a geographical location. It is possible to conceive of other Malaysias, but only one can be brought to fruition without force. Thus, Lee makes it clear that first, "Malaysia" does not yet exist, and second, that "Malaysia" can be one of many possible ideas.

At this point, the speech ceases to be a description of the ideal Malaysia, and becomes a rallying call to all like-minded, peaceable Malaysians to work towards achieving this Malaysia of tolerance, social improvement, quality of life and wealth. It is also a battle cry against poverty, as the "battle will be fought" against poverty and inequality by the innovating Malaysia.

Summary of Analysis

The title of the speech: "Are There Enough Malaysians To Save Malaysia?" highlights and conceptualises the need to hold true to the speaker's ideal of Malaysia, for this ideal is under attack and needs to be rescued from its enemies. Notably, in speaking of Malaysia's enemies, Lee steers clear of metaphors, identifying the enemies clearly – Communism and Communalism. Certainly, this is effective here for it does away with any possibility of confusion.

Notes

1. Tunku Abdul Rahman's separation speech, *Straits Times*, 10/8/65.
2. Nancy McHenry Fletcher, "The Separation of Singapore from Malaysia", Department of Asian Studies (Ithaca, NY: Cornell University Southeast Asia Program, 1969).
3. Fletcher, 3.
4. Dennis Bloodworth, *The Tiger and the Trojan Horse* (Singapore: Times Book International, 1986).
5. Bloodworth, 289.
6. Fletcher, 5.
7. Fletcher, 6.

4. Consolidating And Moving Ahead (1964–1965)

Historical Background

The message to the nation after Singapore separated from Malaysia was one of consolidation and moving ahead. This was not an easy task for the speaker as the year prior to Singapore's separation from Malaysia had witnessed the race riots which claimed 34 lives.[1] These riots were even more prolonged than the Hertogh riots of 1950. Maintaining racial harmony and social integration was thus an uphill task. The hope for consolidation and a united sense of nationhood seemed far away. That Singapore has, since 1965 until today, maintained standards of housing, education, health, savings and income that are the envy of Asian countries and the world is nothing short of a miracle.

The following speech, delivered on the eve of National Day in 1966, is representative of Lee's rhetorical skills, which is marked with an idealism tempered with industry and strategy. He presents the case at hand in vivid terms, strategising ways to overcome difficult storms and charting the course of action that will propel Singapore's relative productivity, worker attitudes and technical skills among the highest in the world. As we will see, Lee uses spatial orientational metaphors to the fullest advantage.

Speech on Eve of National Day, 8 August 1966

Speech

This is a speech delivered by Lee Kuan Yew at the National Day Rally held at the National Theatre on the eve of National Day, 8 August 1966.

Source: *Prime Minister's Speeches, Press Conferences, Interviews, Statements, etc.* (Singapore: Prime Minister's Office, 1966).

Friends and fellow citizens,

This time last year, my colleagues and I had already made a fateful decision on your and our behalf. In the nature of the circumstances, there was no time for consultations. We could not find out what the consensus would have been had we refused to acquiesce and had we insisted on going on with the kind of Malaysia which we envisaged it was, at the time when we agreed to join.

It is useful this evening not so much to go back to the past – the whys and the wherefores – to apportion blame but more to search deep into our hearts to ask if the things we set out to do were right or wrong; were good or bad. And I say that we have no regrets. We are completely unrepentant that we set out to build a multi-racial and, for some time, a multilingual, a multi-cultural community, to give a satisfying life to the many different kinds of people who foregathered here in over 150 years of the British Raj.

And we, in the end, on balance decided to carry on with our multiracial experiment – if you like to call it – just in Singapore alone rather than be forced into large-scale conflict in Malaysia.

Nothing has altered, not the basic data nor our basic thinking.

What has altered are the circumstances in which we now find ourselves.

I think it is reassuring on an anniversary to weigh the odds to see how we have performed, the promises against the performances. And my experiences of Singapore and her young, active, energetic if somewhat exuberant people is that given honest and effective leadership, an honest administration within which to bring forth themselves, they will make the grade.

It has been a year of great and sudden change. Very few countries in the world go through this kind of climacteric we have gone through.

From 1961 to 1963, we fought for merger, to sink ourselves in the identity of a bigger whole. Between 1963 and 1965, we found ourselves gradually embroiled in something which we half suspected but never quite admitted was possible within such a multiracial situation. And in 1965, with decisive suddenness, we found ourselves asunder.

All the while, despite all the political unpleasantness that followed, we were making progress. Imports went up and so did exports.

These are facts and figures, not fictions of the imagination of my colleague, the Minister for Finance. They have checked against every indent that goes in and out of the Port of Singapore Authority. They have checked against our revenue on the same rates of taxation; the number of factories, the people they employ, the goods they produce, their value; the houses being built. And they tell a story which we have very little to be ashamed of. Almost in spite of ourselves, we have forged ahead; revenue has gone up 10 percent; the economy is surging forward.

I am not saying that this will be so far all the time with no effort on our part. But we will progress so long as we reward initiative and resourcefulness; and as long as whenever we face peril, courage and resolve are never found wanting.

But more than just making material progress, like other groups of human beings wherever they are found in the world, we seek permanent salvation, security to time immemorial, to eternity.

We believed – and we still believe – that that salvation lies in an integrated society. I use the word advisedly – "integrated" as against "assimilated".

I would not imagine for one moment a Singapore Government trying to assimilate everybody. You know, 75 percent Chinese trying to convert 10 percent Tamils and Hindus and Tamil Muslims and Northern Indian Muslims into good old "Chinamen" – or not even good old Chinamen: good old "Overseas Chinese", Singapore brand, Singapore type.

I would not try it; it is not worth the effort. Nor would I try it with the other groups. Certainly, not my colleague like Encik Othman who has been here for many, many generations; or even my colleague like Tuan Haji Ya'acob from Kelantan where he was born.

Why should we try the impossible?

But I say integration is possible – not to make us one gray mass against our will, against our feelings, against our inclinations, but to integrate us with common values, common attitudes, a common outlook, certainly a common language and eventually, a common culture.

It is most important that we should understand what is it we are after in the long run. And, if we are after a permanent and secure future for ourselves, then this must be done: to build a society which, as it progresses, improves, flourishes and gives an equally satisfying life to one and all.

If groups are left behind either on the basis of language, race, religion or culture, and if with these groups, the line of division coincides with the line of race, then we will not succeed in our long-term objective of a secure future.

Consolidating and Moving Ahead

For so many other countries in this part of the world are faced with the multiracial societies that gradually formed themselves over the period of colonial rule.

Broadly speaking, there are two ways in which we in Singapore can set the pace.

First, prove that the migrant element is dynamic, is thrustful, is industrious and can get on – of that, I have no doubt – but that in the process of getting on it is unmindful of its wider responsibilities and its long-term interests, leaving in its train a whole trail of frustrations and bitterness which must have its repercussions throughout the whole region as men's minds begin to ponder on the unpleasant consequences of what we have done or what we have manifested.

The other way is to demonstrate that we are a forward-looking, not a backward-looking society, not looking to the past for examples of patterns of behaviour and conduct completely irrelevant in the modern society that we now find ourselves . . . Man reaching out for the moon and the stars . . . It is to show we do not find our solutions by turning over the dusty pages of some chronicle of some ancient time telling us about some ancient customs more relevant to his days, but that we have the forward, the inquiring outlook, and are keen to learn, keen to make a success of the future.

If we can give everyone – regardless of race, language, culture – an equally satisfying life, then surely that must be a benevolent or a beneficial influence on the whole region as other people turn their eyes towards us and say, "It is not true . . . Given the right political attitudes and the aptitudes and the framework of a good, effective administration, all can thrive and prosper."

It is in the nature of things that we must talk in parables. And the older I become, the more I am convinced that sometimes perhaps, the Prophets spoke in parables because they had also to take into account so many factors prevailing in their time. But, I would like to believe that we are a people sufficiently sophisticated to understand parables and the value of ever searching for new solutions, new ways to achieve old targets.

Never be depressed, never be deflated by setbacks. We suffered setbacks: In 1964, there were two communal riots. And we do not pretend to ourselves they were not communal riots – they were. We face facts.

And this is one of the greatest strengths about Singapore: its willingness to face reality including the 9th of August.

We used to celebrate the 3rd of June; then, it was the 16th of September, when we promulgated Malaysia. Then, it went back to the 31st of August because other people celebrated the 31st of August. And then it had to be the 9th of August, and the 9th of August it is, not because we wished it to be but because it was.

This capacity to face up to situations, however intractable, however unpleasant, is one of the great qualities for survival. A people able to look facts squarely in the face, able to calculate the odds, to weigh the chances and then to decide to go it, are a people not likely to go under.

And when this time last year, before the news was broken to the world, my colleagues and I carried that heavy burden in our hearts of having made the decision on your behalf, we consoled ourselves with this thought: that whilst thereafter, the multiracial society that we had set out to create could be implemented only within the confines of Singapore, we knew deep down that ultimately, its impact must spread far beyond its shores.

No geographic or political boundary can contain the implications of what we set out to do when we succeed. And, there is no reason why given patience, tolerance, perseverance, we should not, in this hub, in this confluence of three indeed, four great civilizations, create a situation which will act as a yeast, a ferment for what is possible, given goodwill, forbearance and good faith.

Every year, on this 9th of August for many years ahead – how many, I do not know – we will dedicate ourselves anew to consolidate ourselves to survive; and, most important of all, to find an enduring future for what we have built and what our forebears will build up.

Thank you.

Metaphoric Analysis

This speech offers several areas of analysis for the speech critic. The metaphors used fall into different categories within the framework of metaphorical concepts. These include orientational metaphors as well as structural metaphors of the type that were seen in the earlier speeches.

As discussed in Chapter 1, much of ordinary experience is expressed and thought of in terms of spatial orientation:

> Are we *on* for tomorrow?
> I look *back* at my past with regret.
> It was an *up*beat speech.
> He was *down* hearted.

One observation that can be made from these examples is that metaphors using the spatial orientation of **up**, **forward** and **on** seem to be associated with positive feelings and events, while those using **down** and **back** seem to be associated with the negative. Another observation is that these metaphors are common expressions rather than novel ones. It certainly seems to be part of the convention of English speech that certain spatial orientational terms are used to express the positive, as well as the negative.

The majority of spatial-orientational metaphors employed in the speech can be divided into those that are used to convey a positive experience or feeling and those that convey negative or less satisfactory events and emotions. Positive ones are:

> set *out* to build a ... community, to give a satisfying life,

> to bring *forth*,
> go *through* the ... climacteric,
> *making progress*,
> imports went *up*, and so did exports,
> forged *ahead*,
> revenue has gone *up*,
> economy is surging *forward*,
> what it is we are *after* in the long run,
> we are *after* a permanent and secure future,
> *build* a society which, as it progresses, improves, flourishes and gives ... satisfying life,
> the migrant element is *thrustful* ... and can get *on*,
> *forward*-looking,
> man reaching *out* for the moon and the stars,
> we have the *forward*, the inquiring *out*look,
> other people turn their eyes *towards* us,
> *face* reality,
> *face* facts,
> *face up* to situations,
> look facts squarely in the *face*,
> set *out* to create,
> set *out* to do, and
> build *up*.

The negative expressions are:

> go *back* to the past ... to apportion blame,
> *sink* ourselves in the identity of a bigger whole,
> *embroiled* in something,

Consolidating and Moving Ahead

against our will... feelings... inclinations,
groups are left *behind*,
leaving in its *train* a whole *trail* of frustrations,
backward-looking society,
not looking to the *past*,
turning *over* the dusty pages,
deflated by *setbacks*, and
go *under*.

A closer look at the spatial elements in the positive set of metaphors yields an interesting result. The spatial orientations referred to are:

out (set out to do/build/give/create, inquiring outlook),
forward (bring forth, making progress, forge ahead, surging forward, build a society, as it progresses gives satisfying life, thrustful, get on, forward looking, have the forward, the inquiring outlook),
through (in the sense of successfully enduring in "go through the climacteric"),
up (exports, imports and revenue went up, build up), and
towards (people turn their eyes towards us, face reality/facts/up to situations, look facts squarely in the face).

Thus, it seems that the common concept in these orientational statements is:

Out, forward, through, up and towards are positive.

Since all these directions have in common the concept of going outwards rather than inwards, we can, for convenience and without sacrificing accuracy, summarise the metaphorical concept as:

Outwards is positive.

However, generally speaking, there are other terms employing similar orientations that convey positive experiences and actions.

For **out**, there are, for example, "venture out" and "step out" which both convey a pioneering spirit and sense of firm intention.

For **forward**, there are expressions like "the future *before* us", "I look *forward*", and "the opportunities *ahead*". This tendency to associate "forward" orientations with a positive reaction is, perhaps, the result of our cultural conditioning and even physical reality (after all, our eyes face front, in the direction we pursue).

Similarly, for **through**, in the sense of going through or enduring hardship and coming out none the worse if not better for it, there are many expressions in common use such as "go through a baptism of fire".

For **up**, the list of conventional metaphors is seemingly endless. In talking of happiness we say "my spirits *rose*", of alertness we say "wake *up*", of health we say someone is in "*top* shape", and of power we say we have "control *over* the situation". The reader will no doubt recall the many other **up** expressions in common use.

For **towards**, there are many expressions, especially references to the future or to success, for example, the "*path* to success" and "look *ahead* to" the year 2000.

On the basis of all these examples, we can plausibly conclude that we tend to organise many basic ideas in terms of metaphors that are spatially orientated. The orientational metaphors employed in the speech seem to be part of a somewhat coherent system as there are many commonly used metaphors using the same spatialisations in an equally positive tone. It seems that whether a particular spatialisation conveys a positive or negative connotation is reflective of particular cultures or language users. Further, there is a certain coherence among the positive spatial metaphors used in the speech. They all have in common the root or major metaphor that:

Outwards is positive

and all have in common the concept of moving outwards. We can refine the root metaphor further by acknowledging that all these spatial metaphors have the concept of movement incorporated within them. Thus, we can identify the major metaphorical concept as:

Outward movement is positive.

How does the use of spatial metaphors affect the audience? It serves to reinforce the message that things are looking up and that the future will only get better. A look at the negative spatial metaphors strengthens this conclusion.

The negative metaphors can be categorized as:

> **backward** (go back to the past, leaving in its train a trail, dusty pages of some chronicle of some ancient time, left behind, backward looking, looking to the past),
> **against** (against our will, feelings or inclinations), and
> **down** (sink ourselves in the identity of a bigger whole, embroiled in, deflated by setbacks, go under, be depressed).

The common concept in these orientational statements is:

> **Backward, against and down are negative.**

These directions have in common the concept of going inwards, rather than outwards. Thus, we can, for convenience and without sacrificing accuracy, summarise the metaphorical concept as:

> **Inwards is negative.**

As in the case of the positive metaphors, it is easy to realise that many conventional spatial/directional statements rely on this concept.

For **backward**, we recall statements like:

> *regressed* into a childlike state
> *back* to the drawing board
> *backward* in one's thinking

and not to mention the various insults that have to do with one's behind.

For **against**, there are statements referring to war and argument, eg.

> go *against* an opponent, and
> go *against* the grain (a statement, apparently from carpentry that has found its way into ordinary usage).

For **down**, examples include:

> *down* and out
> *sink* into depression
> *fall* from grace
> the stock market *fell*, and
> the Great *Depression*.

In the speech, as the audience hears the negative statements that rely on the metaphorical concepts of **down**, **backwards** and **against**, they receive the overall idea that relying on the past or even looking at it has little value for Singapore at that point in time. The overall impression is that it is time they look to the future and rejoice in the steps that have already been taken towards realising the future.

In speaking of the future, Lee relies on the metaphor of pursuit. In Lakoff and Johnson's terms, we can call this a "physical" metaphor, where events that have yet to take place are spoken of as being a physical entity or substance that can be pursued. Here, the future is referred to as:

> what it is we are after in the long run,
> we are after a permanent and secure future,
> long term objective of a secure future, and
> man reaching out for the moon and stars.

These convey positive feelings about the future for the audience. Such a view of the future can motivate their actions and set goals that are seen as inherently achievable. The secure future is further reinforced by the metaphors "making progress" and "forged ahead". "Making" and "forged" convey intentionality, achievability and pursuit of an aim.

Why is this such a satisfying speech? Because it captures the mood of the times, and sets the tone for the future.

This mood of struggle and conflict is reflected by the references to *fighting* for merger, being *embroiled* in a difficult situation and finding "ourselves *asunder*" rather than "be *forced*" into "large scale *conflict*". As many metaphors relating to arguments use terms of war such as:

> shoot down one's arguments, and
> destroy an opponent's arguments,

the structural metaphor here is:

Disagreement is war.

The speech does not refer to violence *per se* (except the 1964 riots) but the metaphors of war referring to the disagreement over the vision for Malaysia may strike a chord in the audience who would surely recall the riots of the recent past. They may feel that this disagreement is a metaphorical war that can easily become a literal war. Thus, it was wisest for Singapore to carry on her pursuit of a multi-ethnic future alone.

Another structural metaphor that would strike a chord in the audience is:

A nation's life is a test.

This is conveyed in terms that emphasize end results, such as:

> in the end,
> on balance,
> weigh against,
> how we have performed,
> the promises against the performances,
> make the grade, and
> bring forth themselves

as well as in the references to Singapore's decision to be an "experiment" and in her need to "progress". To convince the audience that Singapore has made the grade and is not fooling itself, the speaker has carefully "checked against" revenue, imports, etc., recalling the familiar classroom activity of putting a check next to or against every correct answer. The nation is doing well in this test as there is "nothing to be ashamed of", again the image of the classroom where one is ashamed of poor grades. The idea is that a nation brings forth itself and gains credibility when it passes the test to make the grade.

What constitutes making the grade? The terms that refer to success seem to identify national morality with national success. Lee first mentions this at the beginning of the speech when he questioned how "right or wrong" and "good or bad" the nation's goals were. As a nation, Singaporeans should have "no regrets" and be "unrepentant", as their aim (what they "set out" to do) was to build a multilingual, multi-cultural community and create a "satisfying life". In summary, it is moral for Singapore to aim to succeed in creating a satisfying life for a multi-ethnic community.

This metaphor works on two levels. The first level is in its appeal to morality. Most people have some idea of personal morality, but few have a vision of national morality. By outlining a vision for a national morality, the speaker in effect unites all those who aim for personal morality.

Second, by structuring the terms for national morality in positive rather than negative goals, the speaker makes national morality desirable. If the speaker had used destructive terminology and said something such as: "We must destroy communalism", the impression created is one of anger and hostility. But by referring to a "satisfying life", the speaker creates the impression that is desirable, peaceable and worthy.

A particularly pleasing feature of this national vision is that this "satisfying life" concerns not only Singapore's efforts to make "material progress", but also her long-term security. In maintaining the theme of a moral vision, the speaker uses terms usually associated with religion, eg.

> permanent salvation,
> security to time immemorial, and
> to eternity,

thereby creating the structural metaphor that:

A nation, like an individual, can work towards a long term hope of success and security.

This metaphor could inspire both the religious and non-religious to nurture and care for the nation when they think of Singapore as a living entity. This means that the audience is invited to think of national success with a degree of hope and seriousness.

The speaker takes care to explain what the "permanent salvation" is – "common values, common attitudes, a common outlook, certainly a common language and eventually a common culture", a society based on integration rather than assimilation, so that all can "thrive and prosper".

Summary of Analysis

The speaker repeatedly draws attention to the fact that he is using metaphorical rather than literal language. He states that we must talk in "parables", as the "prophets" did. These terms further contribute to the structural metaphor:

A nation, like an individual, can work towards a long term hope of success and security.

The speech goes beyond the concept of a moral national vision for material success, a satisfying life and permanent security. The moral nationalism is expanded to include the idea of being a model or example to others. Although the society that Singapore aims to create would be confined to its own shores, its example would be felt by others, and perhaps would even inspire them to emulate Singapore's success. Singapore could thus be a catalyst to the development and growth of other countries, as conveyed by the metaphor of "yeast" and "ferment".

The religious terminology of "parables", "prophets", "salvation", "security", "satisfying life", "eternity" and going beyond "making material progress" appeals to all who have a sense of idealism combined with purposeful pragmatism. The fact that the speaker openly calls the audience to understand his speech as a parable confirms that the speech is intended to work as a metaphor. The audience is expected to "read" in it a call for a national ideal and vision. It is an inspiring invitation to strive fervently and ardently for a worthwhile future together.

This metaphor, together with the spatial metaphors associated with test and war, all point to end results and achievements. This is significant, of course, considering that the speech was delivered at a time when the future of Singapore was uppermost in the collective imagination of the audience.

Notes

1. Richard Clutterbuck, *Conflict and Violence in Singapore and Malaysia 1945–1983* (Singapore: Graham Brash, 1984), 320–321.

5. The Economic Recession & Recovery (1985–1986)

Historical Background

> *"The years ahead will not be easy. The ailments which have afflicted the Western industrial democracies for so many years will continue to cripple the growth of their economies. Just as Singapore appears to have reached a comfortable level in her economic development, the prospects ahead are for more economic storms rather than for calmer weather. The 90s will not be comfortable years for Singaporeans . . ."*
>
> – Dr. Tony Tan, "The Economy of Singapore: Past Developments and Future Prospects", 11 December 1981 at National University of Singapore, published by Information Division, Ministry of Culture

These were prophetic words in 1981. Premonition became reality as an economic recession hit Singapore in 1985. The second quarter of 1985 posted zero growth and 90,000 jobs were lost. Real Gross Domestic Product (GDP) in manufacturing, transport and communications, commerce, financial and business services and construction took drastic downturns.

Economic competition, uncompetitive wages and a lack of investment in Singapore were the contributing factors to Singapore's economic downturn. As a result, in April 1986, the

National Wages Council (NWC) recommended wage cuts and wage freezes for companies that were performing poorly and those that were marginally profitable. The NWC also made recommendations to companies that were performing well to adjust wages. Together with the wage restraint, tax and tariff, and employer contribution to the Central Provident Fund (CPF) were cut, to lower costs and increase productivity.

Inevitably, the general population had to make deep sacrifices. Jobs were lost, workers were retrenched, salaries were decreased and spending and savings were arrested. New graduates found it hard to locate jobs.

The following provides a selective summary about how workers and companies in Singapore were affected by the economic downturn.

In the Straits Times (1/6/85), the Singapore Manufacturers Association (SMA) reported that it would set up a bureau to "help place retrenched workers in new jobs". This was such an enormous task that the SMA "would welcome any assistance that the government or unions could give to set up the bureau".

The building industry was one of the sectors that were badly hit. The heading of a Straits Times report on 3 June 1985 read: "15 Building Firms Forced To Wind Up". This reflected what had happened in the first five months of the year. The bulk of the wind-ups took place in April. The report cited that a well-known company, Civilbuild, which had an authorised capital of $10 million was among those that were petitioning for winding-up procedures. The fact that Civilbuild, a company listed in the "top categories of the Construction Industry Development Board's central registry of builders", was forced to wind-up reflected the enormity of the shakeup. Tough times were taking their toll. The report added that 25 more building firms were facing winding-up petitions, and forecasted that more of the small companies would wind-up. This included building contractors, building material suppliers, renovation contractors and heavy machinery dealers.

In another report (ST, 8/6/85), Smith-Corona announced that 450 workers would be laid off by the end of June 1985. That brought the total to more than 1,000 workers thus far laid off by the American typewriter company. It had also shut down one of its plants in Chai Chee.

Five hundred workers from Emporium Holdings "were given pay cheques and told not to come back the next day" (ST, 2/8/85). Most were sales staff from the 28 stores of Emporium Holdings. Ironically, Emporium Holdings had won a citation as a model employer the previous year.

On 2 August 1985, 680 workers from General Electric (GE) "collected their last pay cheques" (ST, 3/8/85). Even though there were prospective employers waiting at the factory in Boon Keng Road where the workers collected their final pay cheques, the recruiters were selective. The report cited, for example, that Seagate Technology was "looking for 300 female workers below 35 with at least a Primary Six education to work for three months". These prospective workers also "have to be able to converse in English and work on permanent second and third shifts."

The heading of an article in the Straits Times (25/8/85) said: "Cabbies Hit – This Time By Recession". The recession was a double blow to taxi drivers who at that time were already anxious about an impending diesel tax. Now, "one result of the bad times is that more people are turning to buses or cutting down on taxi trips to save money". Because of this sharp drop in the number of passengers, taxi drivers were forced to work longer hours.

Throughout Singapore, many companies implemented wage cuts and wage freezes. In the Straits Times (7/8/85), General Electric (GE) announced that it was "seeking further cuts in labour cost because of the economic downturn". This was in addition to its retrenchment of more than 2,600 workers thus far. Specifically, GE wanted to freeze annual increments for its workers for two to three years. Workers opposed these freezes, arguing that they had already given up their NWC increments. Workers felt that the annual increments should be viewed as a basic component of their salaries. The management of GE countered that workers in Malaysia and Hongkong were cheaper to employ, and stated that Singapore was an increasingly expensive place to conduct business. The economic downturn, no doubt, cast a dark shadow on the competitiveness of the Singapore worker.

The hotel industry was also badly affected. Shangri-La Hotel, for example, imposed a salary freeze on 200 of its workers (ST, 2/8/85). A spokesperson for Shangri-La said:

> In view of the economic slowdown, increasing expenses and decreasing revenue, all companies are forced to look at ways to minimize expenses. As labour is one of the main expense items, this is an area that requires serious attention and consideration.

Workers who had been with the company for more than three years would not enjoy any increments for 12 months, while those who had been with Shangri-La for fewer than three years were consoled with a five per cent increment. Shangri-La explained that those with three or more years with the hotel had previously enjoyed high increments and were paid more than employees in other hotels. On the other hand, the salaries of those with fewer than three years in Shangri-La were equivalent to or less than the salaries of their counterparts in other hotels.

The Straits Times (1/8/95) gave a more serious picture of how the economic downturn affected wage levels. The headline read: "143,000 forego NWC increase", and reported that "25 major trade unions will not press for National Wages Council pay increases for their members this year". This showed that many employees recognized the need to rally round their employers. They recognized that saving their jobs was of primary significance, and that wage increases, though important, was not a point of discussion at that time. This was reflected by gatherings of union members who carried banners announcing slogans such as:

> Jobs First. Pay Raise Later, and
> Workers Make Sacrifices, Management Do Likewise.

Even though many unions implemented wage restraint, union leaders acknowledged that such a move would still not completely stop retrenchment of workers. Wage restraint was, at best, aimed at decreasing retrenchment.

Just two days after the report on 3 August 1985, more unions announced their intention to sacrifice the NWC increases (ST, 3/8/85). This sacrifice further involved 68,000 workers from the public sector. Since many of these workers earned "relatively low wages", remarked Mr. G. Kandasamy, the General Secretary of the Amalgamated Union of Public Employees (AUPE), this big sacrifice was in fact a good portion of their real wages, and not as negligible as indicated by some employers.

In the light of announcements of wage freezes and retrenchments, the media were forthcoming in their messages to calm fears and instill optimism in the people. In the Straits Times (3/8/85), the editor exhorted Singaporeans to "take stock of the present economic slowdown soberly and view it in perspective". He pointed out that as long as we are politically and socially stable, we can view this "recent spate of bad news" as "part of an inevitable cleansing process, out of which we would emerge leaner and stronger". This cleansing process, he added, was transitory and momentary.

The National Day observances in 1985 were marked by sober reminders from government leaders to the nation to be steadfast and patient as the economy experienced slow growth. Mr. Wong Kan Seng, then Minister of State (Community Development and Communications and Information), lauded the NTUC's "gesture in forgoing the NWC increases", and remarked on the maturity of the trade unions in Singapore. Dr. Tay Eng Soon, then Minister of State (Education and Communications and Information), pointed out that Singaporeans could afford to "freeze wage increases as inflation is still low". The challenge now is: "the survival of the fittest", and for workers in Singapore to be productive in order to compete with workers in other nations. In his speech, Prof. S. Jayakumar, then Minister for Home Affairs and Second Minister for Law, "urged Singaporeans to maintain their fighting spirit in the face of adversity". He was confident that the same spirit that helped overcome the crises during the separation from Malaysia and the Communist Threat could also help fight the recession.

On 16 August 1985, Mr. Ng Pock Too, the political secretary of the Prime Minister's Office, in a convention of the General Council of the Singapore Bank Officers' Association (SBOA), urged workers not to look at the current recession as a "devastating experience for Singapore". He compared the nation to a ship, and her workers to the crew and passengers, and emphasized the need to "keep the ship on an even keel and, having the directions right, to ride out the storm".

Mr. Eugene Yap, the then Senior Parliamentary Secretary (Labour and Environment) at the Mountbatten constituency's National Day dinner, urged Singaporeans to be "careful in using the nation's savings as it remains the key to the country's economic health even in bad times" (ST, 17/8/85). Guarding against any suggestion to tap into the nation's reserves to tide us over the recession, he warned that the nation's savings were essential to her well-being and thus must be used carefully.

As with any recession, jobs were difficult to come by. The Straits Times (12/8/85) carried an article about "1,800 Grads With No Work". This was partly due to the sharp increase in the number of graduates. The negative growth rates of the economy had also affected the employment of new graduates. The report indicated that those without work experience were the hardest hit.

The story of how business shrank continuously for one small businessman is perhaps indicative of how businesses in general were plagued by the bad economy (ST, 4/8/85). Businessman Mr. Reg Joseph, owner of six confectionery shops, was forced by the recession to go back to "where he started – with just one shop". While not opposed to CPF, Mr. Joseph felt that one of the burdens that he had to shoulder was the employer CPF contribution. After closing his first outlet which was not as strategically located as the other outlets, he had said: "The most important thing [in retail] is location, location, location, though in bad times, even that doesn't count." He added that workers generally look for a place with the highest remuneration, and so were hard to come by. Mr. Joseph even had to "plead with those selected [workers] to turn up for work".

As wage freezes were implemented, workers retrenched and the CPF rate cut, public dissatisfaction rose. A spokesman for the Food, Drinks and Allied Workers' Union "strongly object[ed] to any employers' proposal to reduce the CPF contribution rate", citing among other reasons that it was a reduction of wages for workers across the board but a "gain for employers at the expense of workers" (ST, 26/8/85). Mr. Victor Pang, General Secretary for the Singapore Airport Terminal Services Workers' Union, wrote to the Straits Times to say that: "CPF is part and parcel of the salary of every worker in the Republic." Indicating that most people had already accepted that there would be no NWC increase at the end of the year, he added:

> Workers have demonstrated their preparedness to sacrifice. Don't make us sacrifice more unless it is absolutely necessary. Bosses must play their part and must also make their sacrifices (ST, 23/8/85).

One employer requested the release of $370,000 in his CPF account to save his company, so that he could avoid closing down his company which would affect "about 100 employees". He concluded: "It is more important that I survive the economic slowdown now, than to live well during my old age" (ST, 5/8/85).

By the third quarter of 1985, some measures had been applied to check the recession – NWC increases were temporarily put on hold, workers were retrenched, and CPF contributions were cut. Most unions demonstrated solidarity by cooperating to beat the recession. At the same time, government leaders encouraged and admonished the nation to sacrifice.

In the light of such a situation, it is interesting to examine the metaphors that were used in public discourse, both in describing the economic predicament as well as in persuading the nation to sacrifice and cooperate. If metaphor is able to stir the imagination and propel the audience towards rightful action, as the author proposes, it would be helpful to investigate which metaphors were employed and how well they worked.

"The Gordian Knot – Is There An Upper Limit To Our Prosperity?"

Speech

This speech, addressed to students of the National University of Singapore, was delivered by Goh Chok Tong at a meeting organized by the university's Democratic Socialist Club, 1 August 1985.

Source: Information Division, Ministry of Communications and Information, 1985.

I want to discuss a subject that concerns you personally – whether there is an upper limit to your prosperity. We can see problems building up. It is my duty to alert you.

If we do not tackle them now, they will become Gordian Knots. As you know, Gordian Knots are intricate knots. There is no way to untie them.

State of the Economy

This is not an academic discussion. The present economic slowdown shows how real the problem is. For the first quarter of this year, our national income increased only slightly. In the second quarter, there was zero growth, perhaps even negative when the final figure is out. Overall, growth rate for the first half of this year was only 1.3 percent. This is our worst performance since we became independent 20 years ago.

More alarming is the speed at which our growth fell. Growth was 10.1 percent for the first quarter of 1984. It dropped to 9.2 percent in the next quarter, then 8 percent, 5.5 percent, 2.7 percent and zero percent. This speed of descent reminds me of a parachutist jumping off an aeroplane and his parachute failing to open. If we cannot open our parachute in time, we will have a hard landing. We won't need a doctor then. We will need an undertaker.

We don't need statistics to tell us how scary it is to fall without a parachute. We can see the sharp drop in property prices. Construction in the private sector has taken a hard knock. Several thousands of foreign construction workers have gone home. And along with them their purchasing power. That is why many hawker stalls feel the pinch.

That is why shops cry for customers. To make matters worse, our neighbours who are also hit by an economic slowdown are restraining their people from spending in Singapore.

Several companies have folded up. Many workers have lost their jobs, including graduates. I am afraid jobs will not be chasing you this year. You will have to search for them.

A leading local bank advertised for 10 officers. Close to 800 graduates rushed for the jobs. Even the Singapore

Fire Brigade is being courted by graduates. The Public Service Commission told me that it had received 74 applications from graduates. This has never happened before.

Election Results Affect Investor Confidence

During the 1980 general election, I said that given the quality of the opposition parties, the loss of a single seat to the opposition would undermine investor confidence. Mr. Chiam See Tong and Mr. J.B. Jeyaretnam scoffed at me, in and out of Parliament. There they were in Parliament and had investor's confidence been shaken? To be expected, they quoted me out of context. My context was the poor quality of the opposition parties and their candidates in the 1980 general election. They also missed my point. My point was that investors would judge the political maturity of a country from the way the people vote. If voters choose a weak candidate with character flaws over a carefully selected People's Action Party (PAP) candidate, then something must be seriously wrong. They must question the maturity of the electorate. Or conclude that the society contains an element of instability.

The opposition MPs laughed at me. I did not bother to put them right. I was waiting for the last laugh. Not that I was going to enjoy it.

Let me tell you that investment commitments in manufacturing for the first half of this year were only half of what we expected. This means fewer jobs in the future for you. This is not a laughing matter. There are many reasons for the slowdown, which are not connected with politics. But election results do affect business confidence.

Importance of Political Stability

Investors do look at the political stability of a country. Of course, they look at many factors before they invest, like the costs of doing business. But political stability is the first thing they look at. They are not going to put up factories, offices and hotels if they are unsure about the long-term security of their investments. To them, a country is simply a platform for doing business. It must be firm and stable. They look beyond one election. Take for example, the hotels under construction at Marina Centre. They take two to three years to plan, and another three to four years to complete. They may need a further ten years to recover their capital. Big investors must look at least 15 years ahead, or three or four general elections down the road. If there is the slightest doubt over a country's political stability within their investment time frame, they will not sink in millions of dollars. Hotels and factories are immovable assets. They cannot be packed into suitcases and whisked away when a country goes down.

Hong Kong

Look what happened to property prices in Hong Kong in 1982 and 1983. Mrs. Margaret Thatcher visited Beijing in September 1982. She could not come to an agreement with Deng Xiaoping over the future of Hong Kong after 1997. The property market collapsed overnight. You could buy a high class office building for a song. Hong Kong does not revert to China until 1997, a good 15 years away. Yet, confidence immediately evaporated. Confidence was the foundation that held up the market. When it went, property prices tumbled. Now that the political future of Hong Kong has been settled, property prices have risen.

BERI

Business Environment Risk Investment (BERI), a California-based investment consultant company, compiled a Political Risk Index for countries of investment interest. It has noted a "rising discontent" in Singapore in its 1985 report. It has shaved a few points off our Political Risk Index. On a scale of 100, we were given 80 points in 1980 and 1981. This was before the loss of Anson. Now, it is down to 76.

Another international economic consultancy firm, Philips and Drew, also noted the "doubts over the future political stability of Singapore". In its March 1985 study on exchange rates for countries in the Pacific region, it cited this as one of the reasons behind some "erosion of confidence" in the Singapore dollar.

People do look closely at our future political stability. Professor Chan Heng Chee confirmed this when I saw her two weeks ago. As you all know, she teaches you Political Science. She had met senior executives of a multinational company in New York recently. This company is here in Singapore. It has expansion plans but is holding them back. They are studying not only the new leaders, but the new generation of Singaporeans. In particular, they want to know whether the new generation Singaporeans and the new leaders have the wherewithal in them to tackle difficult problems together.

It is not just the new generation leaders who are under test. New generation Singaporeans are also under test.

Delicate Transition

We are passing through a delicate period of our history. The whole country is in a stage of transition.

The political leadership is changing gear. The whole country is shifting gear. The younger electorate is pushing out the older voters in voting power.

Conservative Asian values are being rolled back by liberal, western values.

The economy is being restructured. Familiar places of work have become sunset industries. Woodworking, shipyards, simple assembly plants have to be replaced by high-tech industries and brain-services. Older workers are being retrenched. They cannot be easily retrained and refitted for the new high-tech industries.

On the other hand, the younger workers have high expectations. They are used to full employment and constant increases in wages. Are they prepared to lower their expectations to a more realistic level? Are they prepared to forego wage increases, if necessary, in order to compete with Hong Kong, Taiwan and South Korea? We are being put to the test now. Our productivity has not caught up with increases in wage costs. We have become less competitive. There is a recession. Can we tighten our belts and adjust to a leaner time? We may have to forego wage increases for two to three years if things don't improve.

In brief, investors will watch us closely in the next few years. They want to see if the whole country can change gear smoothly. They want to see how we respond to the present economic crisis.

Inherent Instability In Democratic System

We have inherited the parliamentary system of democracy from the British. It is a fair system. It has worked for us, so far. But we must beware its one structural weakness. It does not have stabilizers, like a modern ship, to reduce the roll of the ship in rough waters. The stabilizers minimize the risks of the ship capsizing in a storm. The democratic system of government does not have a stabilizer to steady the ship against waves of popular demands that want to be satisfied immediately. That is why many governments elsewhere roll from left to right, and right to left, every now and then. In Singapore's context, where there is no credible alternative to the PAP, the absence of a stabilizer becomes a design fault of the democratic system.

Japan and LDP

Singapore is not like Japan where there are safe seats for the ruling Liberal Democratic Party (LDP). The rural seats are the strongholds of the LDP. They are the stabilizers of Japanese democracy. Some urban seats may change hands from one election to another. But there will always be enough constituencies to return the same mainstream political party to power. That is why Japan does not teeter and totter from one party to another.

Core of Anti-Votes

In any country, there is always a core of citizens who will vote against the government for whatever reasons. In Singapore, in the 1980 general election, the PAP won 76 percent of the votes. 1980 was a good year for Singapore. Even in a good year, about 24 percent of the electorate voted against the government.

If we take the anti-establishment votes to be, say, 30 percent, the fate of Singapore really rests on only 20 percent of the voters, 70 percent less 50 percent. If there is a swing of only 20 percent, there will be a new government. This is because most constituencies have similar electoral profile. A swing will affect all constituencies. Let me elaborate. Only two constituencies do not have a large HDB population – Joo Chiat and Tanglin. The rest are either fully Housing and Development Board (HDB) estates or have a large HDB component. All HDB constituencies have a representative mix of poorer and better-off Singaporeans. Each of them is a miniature Singapore.

The electorate may be persuaded by populist policies. If that happens, an upset general election result is not to be ruled out. An electoral swing will be across the board. It will not be confined to only a few marginal seats. I think the opposition parties understand the mechanics of democracy and the psychology of voters. That is why they concentrate on fanning dissatisfaction instead of campaigning on alternative programmes and visions. That is why they have never told you the truth about Singapore's basic problems. That is why they have never supported the tough but necessary measures of the government.

I hope the day will never arrive when waiting for the general election results is like watching the flipping of a coin. If that day arrives, then we have reached the upper limit of our prosperity.

Psychology of Voters

Let me elaborate on the psychology of the voters. Let me explain this with the results of past general elections.

General Elections, 1968–84

Year	Total No. of Seats	No. of Seats Contested	% of PAP Votes
1968	58	7	84.4
1972	65	57	69.0
1976	69	53	72.4
1980	75	37	75.9
1984	79	49	62.5

In the 1968 general election, only seven out of 58 seats were contested. PAP received 84 percent of the votes cast. There was a good reason for this. Only months before the general election, the British had announced their intention to withdraw their armed forces from Singapore. Many of you may have forgotten, but there were thousands of British troops in Singapore employing thousands of Singaporeans. Unemployment then was over 10 percent. More importantly, with their pullout, Singapore would be as naked and defenceless as a newborn baby. Nobody other than the PAP dared to take on the job of looking after Singapore. The population rallied behind the PAP.

After the shower was over, opposition parties sprung up in great numbers like mushrooms. In 1972, they contested 57 out of 65 seats. Amongst them was Mr. Jeyaretnam. 69 percent, or more than two-thirds of the population, supported the PAP.

In 1976, the support went up to 2 percent. Note that South Vietnam had fallen into Communist hands only one year earlier. Singaporeans signaled that they wanted a strong government.

In 1980, they increased their support to 76 percent. Again, remember that the whole world, including Singapore, was rocked by the sharp increase in oil prices in 1979. Oil price in the spot market was jacked up from US$19 per barrel to US$40 per barrel.

1980 to 1984 were four of our best years in economic development.

Never had income for our workers gone up so fast. Never had HDB built so many flats in so short a time.

Yet, never did the votes for the PAP fall so low – 63 percent compared with 76 percent in 1980, and 84 percent in 1968.

There are deep implications here for us. Does prolonged peace and prosperity contain the seed of its destruction? Think about it. Have we so quickly forgotten our painful birth and poverty years? Have we reached the peak of our political stability? Are we suffering a rich man's disease? If every general election from now is like flipping a coin, then we have reached the upper limit of our prosperity.

Land and Water

Whoever is in charge of Singapore in the future will have to solve two other problems – land and water. These are not immediate problems. But if we don't attend to them now, it will be too late for a solution in 10 to 15 years' time.

Let me deal first with land. I never realized how small Singapore was until I went down to Australia in 1979. I really felt small when I learnt that many farmers owned cattle farms bigger than the whole island of Singapore.

HDB has built some 620,000 units of flats. The Minister for National Development told me that we only have enough land to build another 400,000 units of HDB flats. On paper, one million units of public housing should be sufficient to house all Singaporeans – three persons to a flat, one million flats for three million people. In practice, homes will not be so neatly distributed. It is likely that some young Singaporeans then may have to buy their flats from the resale market. There will be no new HDB flats to be sold at subsidized prices. Do you know what this means to you personally? It means that if you do not inherit a flat from your parents, you will have to buy one from the open market, possibly, at high prices.

You will begin to feel the pressure of land shortage in eight to 10 years' time. You will have fewer choices of housing estates. Saturation point will be reached in about 15 years' time. After that, there is no more land for new towns.

I now move on to the next potential limit to growth – the continued availability of sufficient water for the population. I believe a person can live without food for 40 days but he will die after four days without water.

Singaporeans happily assume that there will always be enough water for them. They will not be so happy if they know the full facts.

We have two water agreements with the Johore Government, one signed in 1961, the other in 1962.

The first water agreement provides for Singapore to draw water from Tebrau and Scudai rivers. The maximum dependable yield from this source is 138 million gallons per day. This water agreement will expire in 26 years' time.

The second water agreement allows us to draw water from Johore River up to 250 million gallons per day. It will expire in 76 years' time.

The potential upper limit to our water resources is therefore 250 million gallons per day, not 388 million gallons per day, as the first water agreement will expire within our lifetime.

We now use 190 million gallons of water per day. We have been increasing our water consumption at the rate of 10 million gallons per day. At this rate, we will reach the potential upper limit of 250 million gallons per day in six years' time. That is why we are always urging you to save water.

Conclusion

Let me summarize my main points.

We can see problems building up for ourselves. We can see the knots being tied.

We are in a delicate stage of transition. It involves not just the political leadership, but the whole country. Our expectations have increased. Our values are changing. It is not just the new generation leaders who are on trial. Do we have the same courage, guts, foresight, tenacity and the sense of purpose as the older generation?

I do not accept that we have reached the upper limit of political stability.

Neither do I accept the limits imposed on us by land and water. That they are finite resources we must accept. But we can work within these finite resources to maximize our prosperity.

The question which we the younger generation Singaporeans will have to ask ourselves is this: Are we prepared to face up to tough problems together? If we are prepared, we have to swallow bitter medicine from time to time to protect ourselves against diseases. That is what our national servicemen do. They swallow bitter anti-malarial pills when they train in the jungle.

If you are not prepared to swallow bitter medicine, then we live for today. Have a good time together for five, perhaps 10 years. And then take leave of Singapore. The sensible thing for us to do is to recognize the tough problems ahead and cut our way through the Gordian Knots. That is the only way to have a bright and secure future indefinitely.

I have been in politics for nearly nine years now. I now know what the Old Guard mean when they say politics is about the survival of a country and its people. It is not just about ideals. It is also about jobs, homes and security. Our problem is not leadership transition. Our problem is whether a new generation of Singaporeans can overcome new challenges and secure for themselves a better life.

Metaphoric Analysis

Following Lakoff and Johnson's suggestion, it is helpful to group the metaphors in this speech into clusters. The first of these clusters consists of the metaphors:

> Gordian Knot,
> parachute/parachutist, and
> swallow bitter medicine.

The second cluster is made up of the metaphors:

> changing gear/shifting gear,
> tightening our belt, and
> safe seats.

The last cluster of metaphors comprises:

> stabilizers,
> modern ship, and
> rough waters.

Cluster One   The metaphors "Gordian Knot", "parachute"/ "parachutist" and "swallow bitter medicine" can be categorised under the metaphorical concept:

> **Economic recovery is a military strategy.**

Note that the title of the speech itself contains a primary metaphor – the "Gordian Knot". This is a term borrowed from one of the stories about Alexander the Great, whose military prowess is legendary. In 333 BC, when Alexander the Great and his troops stormed Anatolia, they were stopped at Gordium, the capital of Phrygia. Alexander came upon Gordius, founder of Phrygia. Gordius' chariot was tied to the yoke with a complicated knot that could not be undone. Legend had it that this knot could only be untied by the future ruler of Asia. Instead of untying the knots that prevented him and his troops from advancing, Alexander the Great cut through the knots.

It is interesting that the speaker does not assume that his audience is familiar with the "Gordian Knot". He mentions that "Gordian knots are intricate knots" and that "there is no way to untie them". That he does not even mention Alexander the Great or allude to him suggests that he is primarily concerned with the basic point that a "Gordian Knot" is a metaphor for a stubborn barrier that prevents advancement and that the act of cutting through the "Gordian Knot" represents bold resolve and action to tackle a seemingly insurmountable problem. Alexander's bold and aggressive action of cutting through the knots can be purposefully juxtaposed against a more patient and non-aggressive manner of untying the knots. The latter obviously takes too much time and even then does not promise any guarantee of success. After all, the knot may be a dead knot that is impossible to untie. And there is an inherent urgency to cut through the knots. A more practical and expeditious solution is therefore necessary – the act of cutting through it. In Greek and Roman mythology, the sword represents absolute sovereignty and the instrument of rule. To be the master of the intricate knot, the symbol of sovereignty, the sword, is used to break down the obstruction caused by the knot. Thus, the image of Alexander cutting through the knot portrays swift solution of a problem.

There is a difference between a rash reaction to a problem and a reaction that is swift and sure, guided by a strategy. The speaker seems to advocate that the problem must be solved strategically, even though it is to be acted upon swiftly and that it is something that demands careful contemplation. This seems to be the crux of the speaker's argument: he identifies the problem and its causes, and suggests how they can be fixed. Yes, the intricate knots have to be cut, but not without a strategy.

Even a parachutist who urgently needs to reach the ground must strategise. Only at a given time is he to pull the cord; he is to be cognizant of the winds that might sway him off course and of the necessary adjustments that need to be made so that he lands where he wants to. This is no amateur weekend parachutist, seeking thrills. The parachutist is part of a military manoeuvre to try to capture a strategic position.

The speaker emphasizes the danger of a "parachute failing to open", painting a frightful scenario. In a sense, the parachutist is not to be blamed if the parachute fails to open. Perhaps, it was negligently packed by someone else. Even a skillful parachutist would be at the mercy of a parachute that is faulty. Hence, the cooperation of the packer, pilot and parachutist is of utmost importance: one cannot do without the others.

The speaker next compares this analogy to that of the voting patterns of the citizens. It is all right, he says, that there is political opposition. But to offer political stability and thereby, foreign investment, the nation needs to forge that majority consensus. Therefore, it has to put up a united front to support the government. If not, the speaker points out, there will be a triggering effect that might result in an "upset general election". Returning to the analogy, a troop of parachutists aiming to secure a position may be stymied if key parachutists are lost due to faulty parachutes. Thus, the emphasis is on cooperation, putting forward a concerted stance, and employing strategic readiness to cut the grossly-entangled Gordian knot.

The third metaphor "swallowing bitter medicine" completes the metaphorical concept of:

Economic recovery is a military strategy.

The speaker explains:

> We have to swallow bitter medicine from time to time to protect ourselves against diseases. That is what our national servicemen do. They swallow bitter anti-malarial pills when they train in the jungle.

The fact that the speaker provides this rationale in the context of national service preserves the military tone of the metaphor, and makes it part of the larger concept of military strategy that includes the "Gordian Knot" and "parachutist".

The purpose of swallowing the "bitter medicine" is akin to that of the "anti-malarial pills". This analogy is frightening, because the person who catches malaria without the medicine to fight it might die eventually. It therefore implies that economic death will occur if the populace is not willing to ensure political stability.

The medicine is, of necessity, preventive in nature. Unlike its conventional implication, ie. of handling a disappointment over bad news, the "bitter medicine" here serves as a mode of preparation, preventive rather than corrective. In the immediate context, this referred not only to political stability and economic measures, but also the dramatic increase in the nation's water consumption. The metaphor thus is a warning on potential dangers that might put the nation's well-being in jeopardy.

Aside from the martial context, swallowing "bitter medicine" can also be viewed from the socio-cultural point of view. The metaphor suggests that adversity leads to the fruition of a promise, an idea commonly found in Buddhist, Islamic and Christian traditions. The transitory nature of hardship is thus foregrounded against the promise of reward in the future.

To summarize, swallowing "bitter medicine" fits into the cluster:

Economic recovery is a military strategy

because the metaphor is used in the context of national servicemen swallowing it to ward off disease. The implication thus is to encourage the sense of prevention among the audience. Together with the "Gordian Knot" and "parachute"/"parachutist", these metaphors spell readiness and the act of overcoming. The climax or end of preparedness is represented by Alexander the Great's bold and tenacious decision to cut through the knot, thereby fulfilling the saying that the one to do so would be the ruler of Asia. Just as Alexander was successful, the promise that awaits the audience, if they are not averse to swallowing "bitter medicine", is one of overcoming and prevailing over the recession despite what seemed impossible.

The problem with metaphors is that while they require the audience to be creative and imaginative in applying a metaphor, there is the danger that the audience may misapply or over-apply a metaphor in areas unintended by the speaker. The speaker evidently guards against such a danger and does not lose control of the metaphors he employs. He also ensures that the metaphors do not develop to unreasonable or unacceptable lengths. For example, the "Gordian Knot" was originally associated with military aggression over other countries, but this is not the speaker's intention. Here, the metaphor is applied firmly to the case at hand.

Cluster Two   The second cluster of metaphors comprising "changing gear"/"shifting gear", "tightening our belt" and "safe seats" is associated with driving and vehicles, and falls under the metaphorical concept:

The nation is a vehicle.

Although vivid, "changing gear"/"shifting gear" does not specify whether the changing and shifting of the gears is a preparation for slowing down or speeding up. But the audience is not told about the pace or speed that the shifting gears result in, except that it is best if the gears are changed "smoothly". Therefore, the issue is not the speed of change but rather the safety of the people who are anticipating the change. Close to this issue is that of "tightening our belts", ie. of undergoing adversity, exercising frugality or suffering poverty. "Safe seats" and "tightening our [safety] belts" offer protection against unexpected manoeuvres that might have disastrous consequences. With "safe seats" and a gradual adjustment of speed in response to changing circumstances, the audience can manoeuvre a safe course of action.

This second set of metaphors works at another level. Since the speed of travel is not indicated and the destination is uncertain ("investors will watch us closely in the next few years"), the audience is not to presume that their prosperity and economic success is a function of their own will. Since they need to "compete with Hong Kong, Taiwan and South Korea", there remains the inherent possibility that they might not reach their destination even if they shifted their gears smoothly and tightened their belts. But this does not leave the audience dismal; the admonition focusses on the resolve to make the necessary changes and its timing. External factors can wreak havoc on a nation's economy, but implementing and acting on changes at the right time may forestall a host of further problems.

Another implication of the metaphor of the economy as a vehicle is that the vehicle, already bearing the audience as its passengers, is already in mid-journey. This is clearly not the time to say: "Stop, I want to get off." Rather, this is a time that requires the utmost cooperation from every passenger as the vehicle is manoeuvred, as carefully and proficiently as possible, to the desired destination.

Cluster Three The metaphors "stabilizers", "modern ship" and "rough waters" form another cluster to reinforce the metaphorical concept:

The nation is a vehicle.

They reinforce the earlier cluster of "changing gear", "tightening our belt" and "safe seats" with the warning to be prepared for the adversity ahead.

However, this navigational or piloting cluster focusses mainly on the structure of the parliamentary system of democracy. The "rough waters" are domestic and not international, and the "modern ship" is likened to the parliamentary system. It is a good vessel but it may still be prey to a harbour that does not provide a secure dock. While the driver-vehicle cluster permits outsiders to influence its destination (ie. competition from Hong Kong, Taiwan and South Korea would influence local wages), the navigational cluster deals solely with internal stability. Without cooperation, national stability itself may be at risk. Without internal stability, no strategy will work. This navigational cluster is especially apt when we consider that Singapore is an island nation with a busy port.

Summary of Analysis Lakoff and Johnson's method of clustering metaphors under metaphoric concepts enables the person engaged in discourse to use a multiplicity of metaphors so that a collective force is generated. Metaphorical concepts aid the audience in following an argument and understanding the nuances that are sometimes not easily conveyed through literal language.

The metaphors associated with military strategy and vehicle generate the collective force that the nation must not stagnate. It must move forward with deliberate manoeuvring by the leadership, and concerted collaboration by the nation.

"Economic Recovery, Education and Jobs"

Speech

This speech was delivered by Goh Chok Tong to the Singapore Polytechnic Students' Union on 29 January 1986.

Source: Information Division, Ministry of Communications and Information, 1986.

I am talking to you not in the best of economic times. Before us, as a nation, is a big challenge. We are in a recession. To get out of it, we have to take some painful decisions. Are we prepared to take, and accept, the necessary painful decisions to boost investor's confidence, generate new investments, and create more jobs?

Size of Job Loss

Last year, we lost 90,000 jobs. Put in another way, this is equivalent to a school leaver having to wait 4½ years before he can get a job. Let me explain. Every year, we need to find jobs for 20,000 Singaporeans entering the labour market for the first time. These first-timers are mostly young people like yourselves.

Ninety-thousand jobs lost mean 4½ years of jobs lost. We have, however, not felt the full effect of this job 'haemorrhage' – it is like a bleeding from the economy – because most of those who lost their jobs were foreign workers. They have gone home. But, if we don't stop the bleeding quickly, more Singaporeans will lose their jobs – and they cannot go home to somewhere else.

External Factors – Falling Commodity Prices

Whether we can prevent this, however, depends not just on us, but on the world outside as well.

The general view is that 1986 will be another year of slow growth for the major economies, like the United States and Japan. Our neighbours, Malaysia and Indonesia, also do not expect their economies to grow vigorously. They are affected by the low level of commodity prices.

Prices of commodities like oil, rubber, tin, sugar, palm oil, cocoa, indicate the state of the world economy. If they are all falling at the same time, it can only suggest further problems ahead.

Commodity prices have fallen from their peak in 1980, and have remained low for five years now. They are not expected to improve in 1986. We get into a vicious circle here – low prices mean less income for producer countries. Less income in turn means less power to purchase manufactured goods from the industrialized countries. Since demand for manufactured goods is weak, industrialized countries in turn have low demand for commodities, which keeps commodity prices depressed . . . and on it goes.

Petroleum

Take petroleum as an example. Five years ago, crude petroleum was sold for US$36 per barrel. Now, it is going for under US$20 per barrel. Prices have dropped, but the demand for oil has not picked up.

To understand the implication of low petroleum prices better, let us look at the direct impact on Indonesia, and the indirect effect on Singapore. Indonesia is heavily dependent on oil – 60–70 percent of her foreign exchange comes from oil exports alone.

Indonesia produces 1.2 million barrels of oil per day. A drop in oil price of one US dollar per barrel means a revenue loss of US$440 million per year, or about S$1.0 billion. So Indonesia announces an austerity budget for the coming year. She will spend less. Indonesia is hurt by the weak oil market. And we get hurt too because she will buy less from us.

Rubber

The same story goes for rubber prices. In 1980, each kilo of rubber earned US$1.60 for the Malaysians. Now, it fetches only half of that – US$0.80.

When the Malaysians have less money to spend, they also spend less in Singapore.

Economic Interdependence

This is an interdependent world. We buy from one another, and travel to each other's country. When one country is in trouble, its problem has a knock-on effect on others. Our bad economic performance affects our neighbours. Their problems affect us.

Economic Competition

Interdependence does not necessarily lead to more economic cooperation. More often than not, it means competition. We sell to America. And so do Hong Kong, South Korea and Taiwan. We want to do business with China. So do the Malaysians and the Japanese.

The ability to compete in the export market is not a matter of life and death for most countries. For us it is. We are completely dependent on trade for our survival. We are three times more dependent than Malaysia. The value of our trade with the outside world is three times our national income. For Malaysia, the ratio is 0.9. Ours is about the highest ratio in the world. For Hong Kong, it is 1.8; and for Indonesia, it is 0.4.

Let us look at our dependency on the outside world from another angle. Of the goods and services we produce, what proportion do you think is sold outside, and what proportion to Singaporeans? Two-thirds are sold to foreigners and only one third to Singaporeans. Put in another way, in effect, it means that out of every three Singaporeans, two depend on foreigners for a living, and only one on Singaporeans.

Our Wages Are Uncompetitive

There is absolutely no reason why foreigners should want to buy our goods and services unless ours are cheaper and more efficient than others'. We can legislate the minimum wage to be paid by the Singaporean employers, but can we force the foreigners to pay our minimum wage? Obviously not! They will simply buy their goods from where they are cheaper and better.

So, we have to watch our cost of production, and in particular, wages.

Our wages tower head-and-shoulders over our competitors'. Compare the hourly wage cost of our production workers with our competitors'. The wage cost for Taiwan in 1984 was US$1.90. For Hong Kong, US$1.40, and South Korea, US$1.32. For Singapore, it was US$2.37. I find it difficult to imagine that the Singapore production worker is 70 percent more hardworking than the Hong Kong worker.

We have certainly become less attractive to investors than before. The rate of return on private capital used to be in excess of 30 percent. Now, it is below 20 percent.

In 1980, an investor in Singapore could expect a gross rate of return of 33 percent on his manufacturing plant. Now, he would be happy to make 20 percent.

What is even more disturbing for us is the fact that, compared with the OECD countries, we are only marginally more attractive. If we have only a slight edge over these countries, why should the Japanese, the Americans, and the Europeans invest here?

If we want more investments, and with them jobs, we must create the conditions that make it profitable for investors to set up offices and factories here.

Pincer Strategy

Since our costs have become uncompetitive, the least we must do is to cut costs. The strategy for economic recovery is essentially a simple one. But not painless. We are warring against recession and we must be prepared to make sacrifices to defeat it. In our battle against recession, we shall employ the classic military pincer strategy.

We move against high costs by cutting them down decisively. Simultaneously, we move against the contraction in economic growth by investing more in human resources and productive capacity. This two-pronged attack – cost-cutting and more investment – will trap and defeat the recession. Cost reduction will make us more competitive. Investment in human resources will make us more skilled and capable.

The pincer strategy requires effort and sacrifice to succeed. It demands that we go on combat ration for a while. Are we prepared to sacrifice part of our wages, which have become too high, to beat the recession?

Reduction In CPF Rate

There are many areas in which we can beat costs down. For today, let us limit our discussion to wage costs. Here, fortunately, we have had a high savings rate. Had we not saved, 25 percent of wages from employers and 25 percent from employees, we would have little room to manoeuvre now. But we did. So, we have some leeway. We can cut wage costs without materially reducing the take-home pay of the workers. We have this flexibility because of our Central Provident Fund system. In good times, we save – as much as we can. In bad times, we cut back on savings, instead of take-home pay.

What should the rate of CPF contribution be reduced by? In my view, any reduction of CPF contribution by less than 10 percentage points is not meaningful. The Chinese will describe such action as '空雷不雨' (Plenty of thunder but no rain). A 10 percentage point reduction will reduce the hourly wage of our production workers from US$2.37 to US$2.18. This is still 56 percent higher than the hourly wage of the Hong Kong production worker (US$1.40).

To have any impact on cost-competitiveness, we have to cut the CPF contribution by 15 to 20 percentage points. And they should all come from the employers' side, because the exercise is cost-cutting, not giving employees more take-home pay. We should keep in mind the loss of savings to the workers, in particular, their ability to meet their housing installment payments. I think we can settle for a cut of 15 percentage points.

It is a painful decision to take to cut CPF savings by this size. You are not working yet, and may not fully understand the pinch. But your father, or elder brother or sister, will. We have taken a long time to decide over this. It is not a decision which we take lightly, or without regard for workers' welfare. But the choice, in simple terms, boils down to jobs or no jobs, economic recovery or more recession.

Faced with such stark facts of life, we have no choice but to decide on a deep cut in the employer's CPF rate of contribution. It is wiser for us to cut our savings now and keep our jobs than to hang on to our savings and lose both jobs and savings later. When the economic situation improves, we can reinstate the higher CPF rate, step by step, and without upsetting investors' confidence.

Let me caution that even with a bold reduction in CPF, there is no guarantee that we will turn the economy around in a hurry, if the external environment is inhospitable. If world trade does not expand, and commodity prices remain weak, recession may stretch well into 1987.

Confidence In Our National Character

This is our first stiff test since independence. Many foreign journalists are gleefully reporting our woes. One London newspaper headlined a Singapore report this way: "Why Singapore has the shakes," making it sound as if we have contracted AIDS. Well, we haven't . . . and such comments should make us even more determined to overcome our present difficulties. You have a lot of future ahead of you. We will not let you down.

But we must work together to give investors confidence in us.

Potential investors want to know whether Singaporeans can adjust quickly to changes in market conditions. They want to know, when profits are down, whether wages will stay up. By our response, as a people, to hard times, will investors assess our national character. If they find that we are realistic, flexible and resilient in the face of changing circumstances, they will place their money on us. This is our key to generating more jobs. Show the world our toughness. Show them that we can absorb punches.

Education

Now, let me describe the other arm of our pincer. We have the financial resources. We can bring some of our foreign reserves back and invest them in our people.

Briefly, we want to raise the level of education of our entire workforce, and get the habit of continuous learning, continuous upgrading ingrained into each worker.

The old days, when you learned a skill and could count on it for your life-time, are gone. Word processors have replaced copy-typists; and robots, assembly-line workers.

Sophisticated technology has taken away routine jobs from millions of workers all over the world. These workers have either to learn new skills, or take lower-paid jobs, or become unemployed.

Anyone who stops learning after leaving school or graduating is committing occupational suicide. He or she will become obsolete. Any country that does not regularly train and retrain its workers is heading up a blind alley. It will run smack into the wall. Technology is changing so fast and we have to train and retrain, just to stay relevant. Experts in the US forecast that a typical 25-year old engineer will have to be trained eight times within a forty year career, or be out-dated. (I hope none of you thought you'd be safe once you're out of the poly!)

As manpower is our most valuable natural resource, its quality is critical to our long-term economic growth. As a matter of philosophy, we will always invest heavily in education, and continue to upgrade the skill and educational level of our workforce. Better educated workers can more easily be trained to work with greater productivity. They are better able to acquire higher level skills.

We can also use investment in education to help fight recession. We can spend over and above our normal budget to build new schools and junior colleges, upgrade existing ones, and run programmes to retrain our workers. Thus, we convert financial resources into higher human capability.

This is particularly important for us because more than half of our workforce are poorly educated, with only primary or even no education. Compare this with the corresponding figures for the industrialized countries and you will realize how much more potential there is to our workforce if we can only raise this level of education.

In the US, only 15 percent of the workforce do not have a post-primary education. In Singapore, it is 53 percent. In the US, 19 percent of the workforce have a tertiary education. In Singapore, only five percent have a tertiary education.

Educational Level of Workforce

Countries	Primary and Below	Secondary	Post-Secondary	Tertiary
Singapore	53%	31%	11%	5%
USA	15%	50%	16%	19%

Source: Report on Professional and Technical Education, 1985.

Currently, we spend about four percent of our national income on education annually. The Americans and the Japanese spend between six percent and seven percent each year. We intend to increase our expenditure to six percent of our national income. In terms of additional expenditure (expenditure over the present education budget) we plan to spend an extra $3 billion over the next 10 years. Just for comparison, this is 1½ times the amount spent for the development of Changi Airport.

The increased expenditure on education will have two major beneficial effects on our economy. In the months ahead, the construction and upgrading of schools, junior colleges and other educational institutions, will help stimulate the economy. In the longer term, the improved quality of education we can give to our children, will lead to a higher quality workforce, and one that is more able to adjust to rapid technological changes in the world.

This ability to adjust is critical to our survival. Take careful note of this. Whether it concerns wage levels, retraining, or the learning of new skills, we will be swamped by changing circumstances if we do not adapt. Jobs may become obsolete and disappear, but the people who did those jobs will not.

Conclusion

So we have to constantly adapt to changing circumstances to survive. We have an economic recession on our hands, and we have to adjust our wage levels to it. We do not expect the economy to pick up in a hurry, and things will probably get worse before they get better. We must cut our operating costs drastically. Regain our international competitiveness. Make it profitable for companies to operate in Singapore. Attract investors to Singapore. They are the ones who create jobs.

We have fallen behind the others in the international race for investors, and for the export markets. But if we are pre-pared to suffer pain, we can make it to the home stretch. With luck, when the world economy picks up, we will regain our momentum, and with it jobs, and higher wages.

Metaphoric Analysis	A military concept is employed here. While the military metaphor in the previous speech is not overtly stated, the speaker in this speech says that we are "warring against recession". To win this "battle", the strategy is to employ the "classic military pincer strategy".

Again, applying Lakoff and Johnson's suggestion of tracing metaphorical concepts, we can identify a cluster from the following metaphors:

> warring,
> pincer strategy,
> battle,
> trap,
> defeat,
> beat,
> combat ration,
> haemorrhage,
> bleeding,
> survival, and
> adapt to changing circumstances.

The metaphorical concept governing these metaphors is:

Economic stagnation is a martial enemy.

These metaphors are potent because the imagery is vivid. Initially, it might seem that the war against economic stagnation is a bloodless war. But there is a strong implication that people might be hurt because of the "bleeding" and "haemorrhage". In fact, the "bleeding" and "haemorrhage" are already quite widespread – thousands of jobs have been lost. Many families have lost an important source of income. When savings are halted and income is severely limited, life can become unbearable. Since "blood" is often regarded as a metaphor for life, and of course it literally transports and provides nutrients to every part of the body, the loss of a job is spoken of here as a wearing down of life, illustrated by the heavy "haemorrhage". Rapid bleeding leads to death. The answer is not in a transfusion or any kind of medical treatment. The solution lies in fighting back by confronting the enemy and beating economic stagnation.

There is also an implication that this war will be somewhat long-drawn. It will not be soon over. The "pincer strategy" recalls the pincers of crabs. This species moves sideways or horizontally to "advance", conjuring the image of a horizontal movement in order to "move forward". This suggests that the bleeding may continue for a little while longer, as opposed to a "straight ahead" confrontation which may be more rapid. Endurance is thus called for.

Just as a pincer has two parts, the strategy that the speaker outlines is a two-pronged attack – "cost-cutting" and more "investment". These are to occur simultaneously. One aspect of cost-cutting is the adjustment of the employer's CPF contribution. The cutback on the savings as a result of the reduction in the employer's contribution to CPF is akin to consuming "combat ration". "Combat ration" is not exactly the stuff that gourmets crave.

It is tough and unpalatable. It is bland and not particularly attractive. Yet, it is adequate for survival. Consuming "combat ration" for now, the speaker hints, is a prerequisite for enjoying more satisfying meals tomorrow. To allay the fears of the audience, he further hints at the temporary nature of "combat ration" consumption. Yet, he does not specify how long the audience will have to live with the "combat ration". Some wars last for two days. Some, two years.

The other half of the pincer lies in investment. Since this will "defeat the recession", it initially sounds as if the investment is a form of ammunition that will thwart and destroy economic stagnation. But this investment is "in our people", vis-à-vis education and training. This implies that investment is a kind of equipping or armouring against future attacks by the foe – understood to be recession.

Summary of Analysis

Even though the pincer strategy is quite specific (eg. "we have to settle for a cut of 15 percentage points" of the employer CPF contribution), like any battle plan, it is to "adapt to changing circumstances". In a real war, for instance, the weather might influence modifications in the strategy. Likewise, the pincer strategy that the speaker refers to is subject to the global economic climate in general. After all, he says: "there is no guarantee that we will turn the economy around in a hurry, if the external environment is inhospitable."

Even though the contents of the first and

second speeches are rather similar, the metaphoric strategy is quite different. The first speech uses as many as three primary clusters of metaphors while the second speech employs only one. The cluster in the second speech, under the metaphorical concept:

Economic stagnation is a martial enemy

contains as many metaphors as the three clusters of the first speech put together.

A question that may be asked is: "Is it more effective for a speech to contain a single cluster of metaphors or a variety of clusters?" It depends. If the subject matter is new, and its content comprehensive, it might be better to use a cluster of metaphors that will drive home salient points. Of course, it is also worth considering the use of metaphors in relation to the rest of the speech. If the speech is relatively short, it is helpful not to include too many metaphors. On the other hand, when the subject matter of a speech is familiar to the audience, one cluster of several metaphors to underline a thematic unity might be more effective than having several clusters. As the first speech was one of the first major speeches about the future impact of the recession (eg. "we can see problems building up"), it is justifiable that several clusters of metaphors were used sparingly to inform the audience about the dangers of the economic problems and to persuade them to adopt ways to defeat the recession.

"The Second Long March"

Speech

This speech was delivered by Goh Chok Tong at a forum at the Nanyang Technological Institute, on 4 August 1986.

Source: Information Division, Ministry of Communications and Information, 1986.

The title of my talk today is, "The Second Long March". It is inspired by the Long March of the Chinese Communists in 1935. The Long March began in October 1934 at the South eastern corner of China, and ended one year later, in another corner in the Northwest, a distance of about 10,000 kilometres. The Communists, led by Mao Zedong, trekked over endless expanses of very harsh terrain – raging rivers, snow-capped mountains and treacherous marshes. At one point, where there was no water, they survived by drinking their own urine. Of the 90,000 men and women who set out, only 7,000 survived the march. Most of them died from sickness and exhaustion. Only a few were actually killed in battle. For those who survived, it was a real triumph of human endurance and spirit.

One may disagree with the political ideology of Mao Zedong and his comrades. Yet, one cannot help but marvel at the triumph of their spirit over impossible odds.

I feel that the problems we are facing are so complex and immense that they will require strong qualities like those exhibited by the Long Marchers. These are physical and moral courage, perseverance, discipline, dedication, resolution and teamwork.

But when I tested the title on some of my colleagues, they were not the least enthusiastic. They thought the Long March metaphor suggested that I was an admirer of the Chinese Communists. They also pointed out that the Long March was not an all-conquering march, but was, in fact, a hasty retreat of the Red Army.

I looked for alternative titles, like 'The Tasks Ahead' and 'Certainties and Uncertainties'. In the end I felt 'The

Second Long March' was still the most apt. It captures the spirit of determination and toughness of purpose most vividly.

Singapore's First Long March

My Long March metaphor may be inspired by the Chinese Communists but the numerical order is not. I use the word "Second" not after the Long March in China but after a Long March in Singapore. For, in my view, the struggle for survival of Singapore as an independent nation, is also a triumph of the human spirit, a victory of conviction and determination, over impossible odds.

The PAP Old Guard fought the Communists, and defeated them. Our Prime Minister has no doubt that had the Communists won, they would have pulled out his fingernails.

Singapore's survival as an independent nation was also a hard struggle. To begin with, Singapore's birth was not a normal one. It was a painful Caesarian operation, done without anaesthesia. Older Singaporeans were convinced that the new-born Singapore was not meant to survive. But, like a Spartan baby left overnight under a cold open sky, it did.

It is now, of course, history how the Prime Minister and the PAP Old Guard rallied the people, struggled and kept new-born Singapore warm and alive. In retrospect, it looks easy. But at that point of time, nothing was certain.

I remember how the Government flattened the hills and filled up the swamps in Jurong to turn it into an instant industrial estate. I was working in the Economic Planning Unit then. Success was far from certain. For years, Jurong sprouted only a few factories and the Jurong Industrial Estate became known as "Goh's Folly" (not this Goh, but Dr. Goh).

The Second Long March

We have grown up. We will be 21 years old in a few day's time. It is an opportune time for us to reassess and reaffirm certain basic facts and premises before we plunge into adulthood. Where are we heading? What is the landscape like before us?

Singapore is unique as a nation – small, no natural resources, a city-state, a country without a countryside, a nation of many different races and religions. Given these basic facts, Singapore will always be vulnerable to internal and external forces.

Take, for example, the vulnerability of our economic prosperity. I was made vividly aware of this when I first started work in 1964. Trade with Indonesia came to a sudden standstill because of Sukarno's Confrontation against Malaysia. Jobs were suddenly lost. The bumboats were all tied up along the Singapore River. The large number of unemployed youth were described as "the army of the unemployed". When Confrontation ended, and with independence, Singapore grew. It grew rapidly until 1985, when we suddenly plunged into recession. Our economy shrank. Workers became unemployed again. A new army of the unemployed? Of mainly officer grades? We have to worry about creating jobs all over again. Creating jobs and economic growth is, therefore, like climbing mountains. The mountains are always there.

Mountain Ranges

Looking ahead, I can see several other peaks we have to scale. You may say that once you have successfully conquered a mountain peak, there is nothing to climbing the next one. But these mountains are permanently covered with snow, and scaling them is always dangerous, even for the most experienced mountaineer.

At this point in time, we may not be able to plan in detail how to climb since we do not have full information of the topography. But at least we are better equipped than Mao Zedong. What I aim to do in my speech is not to tell you how to climb the mountains, but to outline the obstacles we are likely to encounter. Then I would like to hear your views, after my speech, on how to climb them. After all, the group of Singaporeans who have to participate most actively in the Second Long March will be the young men and women like you.

Physical Constraints on Growth

Our immediate problem is to pull ourselves out of the current economic recession. Our longer-term problem is how to overcome the many constraints on our growth. For example, our land, water and manpower resources are finite, and we are almost reaching their limits. I have spoken on these issues at a similar forum in NUS last year. The Acting Minister for Trade and Industry has also spoken to you on "Recession and Economic Recovery". I shall, therefore, not elaborate on this point tonight. But I want to reiterate that we should go easy on wage increases for another year at least, and to advise you to learn to live with slower economic growth, which means lowering your income expectation.

Human Problems

The constraint of physical resources is not as difficult to overcome as the human resource problem. This type of problem requires us to change attitudes and tread on sensitivities. It concerns people directly. When we deal with people, we are basically dealing with emotions, their hopes and fears, their pride and prejudices, their joys and sorrows. The human resource problem cannot, therefore, be tackled in the same efficient, computerized manner as we can the non-human ones. Unless they are properly handled, any attempt to solve them can itself cause further problems.

People is what makes Singapore. They are our most valuable resource. I think the most serious challenge we are going to face is how to cope with the changing demographic profile – its size, composition and age distribution.

I know this is a longer-term problem but if we do not address it now, it can only become more serious.

Our population now stands at 2.6 million. It will grow to three million in the year 2020, and then decline. Our population will decline because the number of babies born each year in the last 10 years falls short of the number required.

Professor Saw Swee Hock, professor of statistics at the National University of Singapore, has calculated that for our population to replace itself, that is, one person for one person, we required 56,000 babies for 1985. But only 42,000 babies were born last year. There was, therefore, a shortfall of 14,000 babies.

You may think producing babies is the most natural thing to do. But apparently the facts seem to indicate otherwise. It seems that the more we educate our girls, the more reluctant they are to have babies. I do not know whether the reluctance is theirs alone, or whether the boys must also share the blame.

This is not a joke. It is a fact. The girls who have only a PSLE education have no problems. They are producing themselves, one for one. For a population to replace itself, on average, each girl must produce another girl. The girls with an 'O' level certificate or above are not doing that. They are underproducing by as much as 40 percent.

So, here we have the nub of the problem.

Prosperity

We have to pay close attention to the trend and pattern of births because of their consequences on our prosperity and security, in fact, on our survival as a nation. You may be puzzled as to why having fewer babies can result in a less prosperous nation.

Let me explain. Economic growth comes from two sources: growth in the size of the workforce and growth in its productivity. Productivity itself depends on the ability of the population. If the workforce does not increase, then productivity must increase to generate economic growth. But there is a limit to productivity growth as the economy becomes more developed. The Japanese are a highly productive people. Yet in the last twenty years, their growth has not exceeded four percent per annum. The Japanese are good. Do you think we can do better? I doubt. It would be extremely difficult to do better than the Japanese people.

Not Enough Young Workers

Economic growth will slacken for another related reason. With fewer babies each year, the proportion of younger people in the population will become increasingly smaller. Put in another way, our workforce will become increasingly older. Today, the average or median age of our workforce is 31, that is, half the workforce is above this age, and half below it. It will go up to 35 years by the year 2000, and then 43 years by the year 2030.

Will our workforce be vigorous and dynamic? Will investors be attracted to a country which does not have enough young workers? Even now, you can see that many companies prefer to employ younger workers. Not only are they cheaper to employ, but they are also more nimble with their hands, and are more up-to-date in their skills and training.

Aging Population

Our changing demographic profile will throw up another grave problem – how to cope with a fast-aging population. At present, there are about 200,000 people aged 60 or above. The number will quickly increase to over 300,000 in 15 years' time. It will balloon to 800,000, 30 years later. You will be amongst those 800,000 people.

How are you going to support yourselves when you are no longer working? You may say that your children can support you, but bear in mind, at the rate we are going, that many Singaporeans will have only one or not even a single child in their life time.

The older population that is without a steady income will need medical care, housing and to move around. These services will have to be paid for, not by the Government, but by those who are working. Singapore has no natural wealth. The only way for the Government to raise the required revenue to take care of the older population is to levy more taxes on those who are working. And they will squeal. The tax burden can be extremely heavy if it has to support some 30 percent of the population who are over 60 years old.

How do we reconcile the interests of the young and the needs of the old? How do we solve the dilemma? I hope you will tell me later.

Security

I now move on to explain the effect of fewer and fewer births on security.

Put simply, there will not be enough young men to defend the country. We have already extended reserve service to 13 years. Do we extend it to 20? Does it really solve our problems even if we do? Do we enlist girls for national service?

Security is a perennial problem. It is another one of those perennially snow-capped mountains.

You cannot assume that once you are born a Singaporean, you will always remain a Singaporean.

Let me illustrate this point by giving you a bit of my personal history.

I have changed nationality many times.

I was born a British subject. Before I could even walk, the Japanese dropped their bombs on Singapore. Soon Singapore fell, and I became, I suppose, a Japanese subject. The Japanese lost the war in 1945. Singapore was returned to the British, and I became a British subject again. In 1959, when I was still in school, I became a Singapore citizen. In 1963, when I was in university, I became a Malaysian when Singapore became part of Malaysia. Two years later, soon after I started work, I reverted to Singapore citizenship. So, all in all, I have changed nationality five times! I hope there will not be a sixth time.

What I am talking about is our ability to defend ourselves in the future. You may not realize it, but it takes 20 years to produce a soldier – 18 years to grow him and two years to train him.

What Can Be Done?

What can be done? What should be done?

Does the solution lie simply in exhorting our people to produce more babies? Who should do the producing? How do we get those who can afford and should have at least two children to have at least two children? Do we change our family planning policy of "Two is Enough" to "Three is Better"? This matter has to be carefully considered, because by trying to check the anticipated population decline, we may overshoot the target. Then we will have the reverse problem of having too many people on too small a piece of land.

National Harmony

The problems I have raised today are not really new. But like the mountain ranges in front of Mao, we have to cross them, again and again. Each crossing is always difficult, always tricky, always perilous. It requires unity of mind and singleness of purpose. It requires us to work in harmony.

National harmony is absolutely crucial for us to conquer our problems. A country at peace with itself can achieve many things. A country at odds with itself will lose everything. I can think of no better example to illustrate this point than Sri Lanka.

I have been to Sri Lanka several times. I have some friends there. It is, therefore, with some concern that I see what is taking place there.

Some years ago, when I was in Colombo, they showed me their proposed economic zone. They were going to model it on the Jurong Industrial Estate. As recently as a year ago, Air Lanka advertised in our press and on SBC: Come to Sri Lanka for "A Taste of Paradise". Today, investors are not going. Neither are the tourists. The violent disharmony between Tamils and Sinhalese is keeping them away.

The Sri Lankans are not an unintelligent people. Our Senior Minister came from Sri Lanka. Their Minister for National Security (Mr. Lallith Athulathmudali) taught law in Singapore. He has also taught my wife. They have a high rate of literacy. They also practise democracy.

It is not that they do not know that national harmony is important. Everybody knows that national harmony is crucial to progress. But it does not follow that just because you know that it is important that there will be national harmony. It depends ultimately on the politics of the country, its government, and its ability to get the people to work together.

Our Mission

The time has come for our generation to work together, to face the future together, to shoulder the responsibilities of State, and to keep Singapore going. We have already begun our Long March. We will face our share of adversaries and our own mountains. We have to call on our own skills, resolve and courage to overcome them. The problems are great because besides the basic internal problems I have discussed, there will be external pressures and uncertainties. For one, the world is becoming more protectionist and more competitive. Making a living is going to be tougher. For another, the whole Southeast Asian region is undergoing a political change. And change invariably means uncertainty.

The older generation of Singaporeans have marched together to overcome their problems. Our generation must likewise march together to overcome ours. Only then can we cross our mountains successfully.

I have discussed only some of the problems today, like physical resource limitations, declining number of births, particularly by the better-educated girls, and aging population. There are many more. Besides mountains, there are ravines, gorges, landslides, flash floods, and swamps we have to contend with.

Singapore's problems are unique. We can look at other countries which are facing similar problems and get some ideas on how we can approach or tackle ours. But, finally, because of our unique circumstances, we will still have to find our own unique solutions to our own set of problems.

You will notice I did not attempt to offer any solution. The reason for my not doing so is simple. When you go mountaineering, every climber must play his part. You know it is a risky venture. You have to take precautions, like linking the climbers with a rope tied round their waists, for mutual support in case one slips. If one slips or stumbles, one will be saved by the others. The climbers work as a team. They place their trust in one another. We are going to climb the mountains together, and I want to know how you think we can conquer them.

Metaphoric Analysis

The analysis of the third speech will first address another aspect of metaphor, allusions, before the metaphorical cluster is considered.

Arthur Danto uses the phrase "metaphoric pragmatic" to refer to how quotations function like metaphors in a discourse. Even when a quotation does not contain a metaphor, it may work in ways similar to a metaphor, to effect certain ends. Allusions too, have metaphoric pragmatics. Like quotations, they are not traditional metaphors. But quotations and allusions act like metaphors.

"Allusion" is the oblique but identifiable reference to words or phrases from some other text. Allusion is not literal as it may diverge from the language and syntax of the source. This speech makes several allusions to what history books refer to as the Long March of the Chinese Communists in 1935.

The allusive reference can play a similar role to metaphor. The reference chosen is likely to be familiar to the audience, or at least the speaker would assume it to be so. Just as the conceptual metaphor reveals his thought processes or certain aspects of the social milieu, so too the source of the allusion can reveal something of his rhetorical intent.

The allusion has a metaphoric pragmatic if it is seen as establishing some parallel between the situation it is applied to and the situation in the original source of the allusion. The allusion thus takes on a different role from what it had in its original context. As Danto puts it:

> Let Q be a quotation [or allusion], and let F be a function from Q onto some proposition P when the speaker means for his audience to recognize that when he utters Q he means P.[1]

Thus, the audience grasps that they are to see Q as P. This is the intensional use of allusion, to see the immediate context in a certain light, from the perspective of a different situation, and not just to communicate what the reference says. Recalling the interaction theory, Q would be the vehicle and F the metaphorical impact, such that aspects of Q would be applied to the tenor, i.e. the current situation P. This is true whether the quotation (or allusion) is from a separate source or a repetition from another part of the same text.

Alluding to a recognized situation possesses a metaphoric pragmatic because the allusion functions similarly once the audience realizes that the allusion invites them to recognize the parallels between the original situation and the current situation. If the audience has grasped and accepted the parallels between the allusion and the current situation in which it is used, it is immaterial if the allusion was inaccurate in the first place. The audience and the speaker have come to an understanding of what is meant.

Danto stresses the intensionality of metaphors and quotations.[2] He notes that a speaker's intention when uttering a quotation is for the audience to discern the function F with which to work out the final proposition P. This dependence on the reader's ability to recognize and participate in the full working out of the metaphoric pragmatic is just as true for allusions. Similarly, the audience participates in the functioning of metaphors by allowing the conventions associated with the vehicle to interact with those associated with the tenor, ultimately coming up with a final intended idea or complex of ideas. The audience chooses the relevant associations, depending upon their perception of the context in which the metaphor or allusion is used. The speaker, in his turn, relies on the reasoning response of the reader and does not expect a passive reader.

The audience has a choice, upon encountering an allusion, to complete the rhetorical act in different ways, depending on the context in which it is used. However, just as with metaphors, convention ensures the completion of the rhetorical acts in particular ways. The speaker's knowledge of the social and cultural milieu of the audience determines the choice of the allusion to guide them to the conclusions he might want them to draw. The allusion need not tell one how to respond or feel. The members of the audience in effect persuades themselves. They come to see as the speaker does that the two situations can be seen as part of the same schematized structure. They may even identify with the attributes of a character in the allusion or identify his situation with that of the allusion.

Metaphors have a referential status. They refer to, or depict a particular reality or situation. Similarly, allusions depict original situations in terms of its atmosphere and context. Yet, the allusions take on a unique meaning specific to the new context. Thus, the sentence is about the new context and not about the original context.

The new sentence may show agreement with the content of the allusion. This forms the cognitive or explanatory content. So the sentence in the text does not rely only on the authority of the original context to command agreement from the listener. Although this affective element may be present, the content of the allusion is presented as the object of belief or truth value of the new statement. Thus, the allusion, like a metaphor, engages the audience as well as characterizes facts and their interrelations.

The metaphoric pragmatic of the allusion depends on two factors:

1. The speaker expects the audience to recognize the original source and context of the allusion, and
2. The audience is expected to see the parallels between the original context and their own situation.

By calling his speech "The Second Long March", the speaker alludes to the Long March of the Chinese Communists in 1935. He does not assume that the audience knows all the details of the Long March, and so provides specifics such as when the March took place, who led it, what the nature of the March was, how many people were involved and how many survived. He is also careful to stress the aspect of the Long March on which he wants the audience to contemplate and capture, specifically "the spirit of determination and toughness of purpose" of the Chinese Communists. Careful not to mislead the audience into thinking that he is espousing the ideology of the Chinese Communists, he reminds them that his choice of metaphor is limited only to its reference of the "real triumph of human endurance and spirit". Thus, the audience is encouraged to emulate the tough vigour and endurance of the Chinese Communists, not their ideology.

The speaker identifies the First Long March of Singapore as the era from when the PAP Old Guard defeated the Communists. This is a timely reminder of the struggles of the past. At the same time, it reminds the audience that Singapore's First Long March had been a successful one due to the "physical and moral courage, perseverance, discipline, dedication, resolution and teamwork" of the "marchers" of the PAP Old Guard.

The Second Long March is just about to begin. The speaker challenges his audience to overcome the peaks and mountain ranges of this march. The implication is that the audience must exhibit the same qualities as the "marchers" of the previous generation.

It is interesting that the speaker tested the title of the speech on his colleagues and that he considered alternatives such as "The Tasks Ahead" and "Certainties and Uncertainties". Although his reason for settling on "The Second Long March" is because "it captures the spirit of determination and toughness of purpose", students of rhetoric and persuasion would justify the choice of title on other grounds as well. The use of a title that refers to what history texts call the Long March of 1935 enables the speaker to tap into certain aspects of that original Long March which may be known to the audience. The speaker is then able to tell the audience exactly what elements of that original situation are to be applied to Singapore's Long March of the 60s. Thus, here, the use of allusion as a metaphor has advantages over a fresh new title as a new title would not evoke any recollection of the "spirit of determination and toughness of purpose" that may reside in the audience's memory.

Another advantage of using the term "Long March" as an allusion to the work of the PAP Old Guard is to draw attention to the difference in outcome between the Chinese Communists' Long March of 1935 and Singapore's Long March three decades later. In both cases, there was a "triumph of the human spirit", but the audience cannot help recalling that the Communist Long March had been a hasty retreat while Singapore's First Long March had undoubtedly been "a victory . . . over impossible odds".

Having thus recalled the relevant memories for the audience to focuss on, this speech is able to proceed to its actual intention. The speaker continues the metaphor of a march by his references to the changed terrain. There is a brief reference to how the physical landscape had been changed by Singapore's First Long March, in terms of flattened hills and reclaimed swamps in Jurong. This physical change of course represented the last changes in many aspects of Singapore that enabled industrialization and progress to take place. In a sense, the change in physical landscape represented the changes in the nation's outlook and approach to national development.

Then, on an almost poetic note, the speaker asks the audience to contemplate the future landscape. Again, there is a reference to the physical limitations of size and resources. But new peaks and mountain ranges have now sprung up in the form of new economic challenges. Just as the hills of Jurong had had to be physically razed in the First Long March, these mountainous economic challenges would have to be somehow conquered.

The Long March metaphor continues in the reference to peaks that have to be scaled. These new peaks in the Second Long March are not a mere repetition of those in the First March. Because they are different, a new approach is required. The speaker effectively conveys this idea by saying that these new peaks are permanently snow-capped and thus dangerous.

In outlining the obstacles to be encountered

in the Second Long March, the speaker calls for new ideas and methods, for he is aware that the participants in this march are a new breed of "young men and women" — not the "older generation of Singaporeans" who had marched earlier.

In the midst of the metaphor of the march, the speaker makes a second allusion, this time to Sri Lanka. As in the allusion to the Long March, the speaker makes clear that there are certain similarities but there must also be differences. Like Singapore, Sri Lanka has highly-educated people with a vision for their future. The speaker emphasizes the similarity further by referring to how Sri Lanka intended to learn from Singapore's industrialization, just as Singaporeans had learnt from Sri Lankan teachers at the university.

However, the point of difference is that Singapore has achieved and held fast to national harmony. The people work together. This stress on the importance of working together now ties in with the Long March metaphor which reaches fruition with the reminder that mountain climbers need to be linked with a rope for mutual support and concerted effort before the mountain peak can be conquered.

Summary of Analysis

The allusion to the Long March carries metaphoric pragmatics. The task of allusion itself is a metaphorical act, coaxing the audience to see A as B, and to identify properties common in A and B. The common denominator in the Long March in China and Singapore's First and Second Long Marches is clear — namely, the tenacity, determination and resilience of the people.

Within the metaphoric pragmatics of the allusion to the Long March, the method of employing a cluster of metaphors is used. All the references to:

> hills,
> swamps,
> industrial estates,
> landscape,
> climbing mountains,
> peaks . . . to scale,
> conquer a mountain peak,
> topography,
> mountain ranges,
> crossing,
> ravines,
> gorges,
> landslides,
> flash floods,
> mountaineering,
> climber, and
> mission

work together to reinforce the metaphorical concept:

> **Singapore's progress is a Long March over perilous terrain.**

The second allusion, to Sri Lanka, does not use a supporting cluster of metaphors. Nevertheless, it possesses metaphoric pragmatics. It functions like a metaphor for Singapore, in having certain points of similarity, yet showing where Singapore is to be unlike Sri Lanka. The emphasis on harmony and working together in the second allusion dovetails with the Long March metaphor's emphasis on individual responsibility, mutual cooperation and determination.

Notes

1. Danto, 183.
2. Danto, 179 and 183.

Conclusion

This study has explored some of the ideas about metaphor suggested by Black, Lakoff and Johnson, and Danto. In studying the metaphors in the speeches on the various crisis and recovery periods of Singapore's history, some interesting observations can be made.

First, the discovery and analysis of recurrent metaphors can help guard against being distracted by a secondary and minor metaphor. A reading for metaphoric clusters draws attention to what the various sections have in common and how a metaphorical concept unites various parts of a speech. A speech can thus be seen as a unified whole as a forest, not a confusion of trees. Looking at the metaphorical lexicon enables us to affirm the existence of a variety of trees as well as the "big picture", or forest. For example, "parachute"/"parachutist", when viewed by itself, may refer to a weekend hobbyist. But seen with the other metaphors under the same cluster, it is clear that the "parachute"/"parachutist" is part of a military manoeuvre.

Second, metaphor is not a static, inert entity that produces a predetermined result. Even metaphors that have previously been used can be used again for a new persuasive context. Rather, metaphor is a tool with great potential and variation. For example, it is difficult to see how metaphors such as "bleeding" and "combat ration" could fit into a discourse on economic recession and recovery, especially in contrast to speeches that report statistical data and nothing else. But these metaphors work in concert with other metaphors under the metaphorical concept:

Economic stagnation is a martial enemy.

The fact that the economic recession can be overcome by strategy, sacrifice and resolve allows the metaphoric concept to go down well with the audience.

Another observation underscores the fact that metaphors do not come in expected packages. The allusions to Cuba, Hainan Island and the Long March of China function metaphorically. In the "Second Long March" speech, for example, the emphasis on the people's "spirit of determination and toughness of purpose" helps the audience see similarities between the allusion and the "Second Long March".

When used aptly, metaphors serve to inspire. They garner the collective will of the audience and translate it into action and attitudinal change. Metaphors encapsulate complex ideas and assist in their communication. When metaphors are vivid, they provide a reference for the audience to remember. The audience goes away with a picture that remains in the mind's eye long after specific details and data have been forgotten. Also by drawing on common experiences, eg. military experiences, an inspiring bond is forged between the speaker and the audience and among members of the audience.

To avoid studying metaphors in a text is to ignore the fact that metaphors are an integral element of any speech or text, chosen by the speaker or author to communicate with the audience. Analysing metaphors in a text will help us understand how a speaker attempts to persuade an audience through the use of familiar metaphors that excite and capture the imagination.

Index

allusion 32, 33, 93, 169–174, 176–178
antonymic expression 53, 62
Aristotle 1–5, 15, 25, 35, 37

Beardsley, Monroe 14, 36
Black, Edwin 17, 37
Black, Max 10, 13, 14, 16, 28, 29, 36, 37
Batista, Fulgencio 94
Bay of Pigs 94
Bloodworth, Dennis 68, 99

Castro, Fidel 94
Central Executive Committee, PAP 40
Chang Yuen Thong 61
Cicero 4, 5, 35
Clutterbuck, Richard 118
comparison view/theory 24–27
Cuba 93–95

Danto, Arthur 14, 21, 31, 32, 36, 37, 38, 169–171
diaphor 23, 27–28

Edie, James 6, 8, 10, 35, 36, 37
epiphor 23–24

Fang Chuan Pi (see PLEN)
Fletcher, Nancy M. 67–69, 99

Goh Chok Tong 128ff
Goodman, Nelson 15, 36

Hainan Island 74, 95
Haynes, Felicity 25, 37
Hegel, G. W. F. 7, 35
Henle, Paul 26, 36, 37
Hertogh riots 100
Hobbes, Thomas 6–7, 11, 12, 35, 36
Hock Lee riots 40

imagination 29–31
   role 30
intensional/intensionality 31–33, 38, 169–171
interaction view/theory 28–31

Jakobson, Roman 23, 28, 37
Jayakumar, S. 125
Johnson, Mark 16, 18, 21, 25, 34, 37, 138
Joseph, Reg 126–127

Kandasamy, G. 124
Kant, Immanuel 32, 37

Lakoff, George 18, 21, 34, 37, 138
Lee Kuan Yew 40–118
Lim Chin Siong 40
Locke, John 7, 35
Loewnberg, Ina 15, 36

Marshall, David 43
metaphor 1–35
  dead 14–17
  orientational/spatial 18–21, 101, 106–118
Metaphoric pragmatic 32, 55, 62, 64, 93, 169–171
Metaphorical clusters 169, 177
metonymy 23, 29, 38
Mill, J. S. 7, 36

Nietzsche, F. 9–10, 11, 36
Ng Pock Too 125

Ogden, C. K. 10, 36
Ong Eng Guan 42

Pang, Victor 127
People's Action Party 40–60, 65–66, 69
Plato 25, 37
PLEN 40–42, 60–66

Quintilian 4–5, 35
quotation 32, 33, 169, 170

Rajah, T. T. 42
Riceour, Paul 16, 28, 37, 38
Richards, I. A. 10–13, 14, 36
Rousseau, J. 8, 36

Snell, Bruno 25, 28, 37
substitution view/theory 24–27

Tan, Tony 119
Tay Eng Soon 125

Toh Chin Chye 43
tenor 13, 39
Tunku Abdul Rahman 42, 67, 68, 99

vehicle 13, 39

Wheelwright, Philip 23, 28, 37
Wong Kan Seng 125
Workers' Party 61

Yap, Eugene 126